PRAYERS

FOR SUNDAYS AND SEASONS

PRAYERS

FOR SUNDAYS AND SEASONS

◆

YEAR B

PETER J. SCAGNELLI

LITURGY TRAINING PUBLICATIONS

Acknowledgments

Excerpts from the *Revised Common Lectionary* copyright © 1992, Consultation on Common Texts. Reprinted with permission. All rights reserved.

Excerpts from the English translation of *The Constitution on the Sacred Liturgy* © 1963, International Committee on English in the Liturgy, Inc. (ICEL); excerpts from the English translation of *The Pastoral Introduction to the Order of Mass* © 1994, ICEL. All rights reserved.

Copyright © 1996, Archdiocese of Chicago: Liturgy Training Publications, 1800 North Hermitage Avenue, Chicago IL 60622-1101; 1-800-933-1800, Fax 1-800-933-7094. All rights reserved.

This book was edited by Victoria M. Tufano with the assistance of Gabe Huck. Pedro A. Vélez and Theresa Houston were the production editors. The book was designed by Jill Smith, whose design was executed by the production artist, Jim Mellody-Pizzato. This book was set in Goudy and Tiepolo and printed by BookCrafters in Chelsea, MI. The cover was manufactured by Thiessen Printing Corp., Chicago, IL.

Cover art: The image on the cover is taken from an Irish quilt pattern found in the book *Visual Elements* by Rockport Publishers.

Library of Congress Cataloging-in-Publication Data

Scagnelli, Peter J.
    Prayers for Sundays and seasons. Year B / Peter J. Scagnelli.
       p.   cm.
    Includes bibliographical references.
    1. Prayers. 2. Church year. 3. Catholic church — Liturgy.
  I. Title.
  BX2015.68.S29   1996
  264'.13 — dc20   96-34767
                                       CIP

ISBN 1-56854-112-0
PRAYSB

Dedicated

to

The Rev. Dr. Horace T. Allen, Jr.

Minister, Boston Presbytery, United Presbyterian Church (USA)
Professor of Worship and Preaching, Boston University School of Theology
Cochair, English Language Liturgical Consultation (ELLC)

In recognition of his work as
teacher, author, preacher
and promoter of the *Revised Common Lectionary*

Ut omnes unum sint

Table of CONTENTS

◆

INTRODUCTION

Sacred scripture is of the greatest importance in the celebration of the liturgy. For it is from it that lessons are read and explained in the homily, and psalms are sung. It is from the scriptures that the prayers, collects and hymns draw their inspiration and their force, and that actions and signs derive their meaning. Hence in order to achieve the restoration, progress and adaptation of the sacred liturgy it is essential to promote that warm and lively appreciation of sacred scripture to which the venerable tradition of Eastern and Western rites gives testimony (Constitution on the Sacred Liturgy, *Sacrosanctum Concilium*, 24. Second Vatican Council, 4 December 1963).

Prayers for Sundays and Seasons is a companion and resource for all whose worship and witness center on and find nourishment in the word of God proclaimed on the Lord's Day in the midst of the assembly.

For many Western Christians, weekly proclamation is shaped according to an ordered schema arranged in a three-year, recurring cycle called the *lectionary*. Technically, the lectionary is not a book but a table of scripture readings. For ease of proclamation, however, the readings specified in that table have been excerpted and arranged for reading in volumes called lectionaries. But whether using a lectionary book or pulpit Bible, Sunday by Sunday, week after week, Roman Catholics and Reformed Christians, Anglicans and Free Church members, local assemblies that are part of a universal or national church as well as independent faith communities — a widely diverse array of worshipers from remarkably divergent liturgical traditions — are reading the same scriptures. For many of these people, the Sunday proclamation of the word leads immediately and regularly to the eucharistic table. For others, this movement is less frequent or even seldom the case, and interpretations of exactly what happens at that table might be moderately or even radically different.

Nevertheless, though not yet united at the eucharistic table, these Christians are united at the table of God's word. Not yet enjoying full communion *in sacris*, this increasingly large number of Christians has already reached full communion *in verbo*. Because of this basic unity around the word of God, *Prayers for Sundays and Seasons*, though coming from the Roman Catholic tradition, is a practical handbook of public and personal prayer for all these Christians. Because, increasingly, it is the lectionary that shapes our public and personal prayer, Christian prayer life has become again, at the dawn of the third millennium, what it was for our Jewish forebears and for our apostolic ancestors: scriptural liturgical prayer.

What Is Scriptural Liturgical Prayer?

In a now famous quotation, which represented the full flowering and solemn confirmation of more than a century of scholarship and research, the Second Vatican Council called the liturgy "the summit toward which the activity of the church is directed; it is also the fount from which all her power flows" (*Constitution on the Sacred Liturgy*, 9). Far from being a weekly obligation or an exercise of private devotion, the Lord's Day liturgy is placed again by the Council where for centuries it was, and where from the beginning it was meant to be: at the heart of the believer's personal and public life.

To the Lord's Day assembly and altar, believers were to bring all the stuff and substance of their lives lived "in the world but not of the world" (John 17:16), compelled to that liturgy not only for renewal and rest but for intercession and consecration. From the liturgy, believers were to draw strength for selfless love in marriage, family and friendship; integrity in business, labor and politics; zeal for transforming society, and for resisting and reversing oppression. Christians found in that liturgy, in the word and food of the Lord's Day assembly, the courage to bear witness, in the coliseum and the concentration camp, to the Lord Jesus, who had told them not only, "Do this in memory of me" (Luke 22:19) but also, "Greater love than this no one can have: to lay down one's life for one's friend" (John 15:13). In fact, when troublesome presiders have dared to comfort the afflicted and challenge the comfortable, worldly powers have attempted to silence the whole community by murdering those preachers at the altar, during the liturgy, from Archbishop Thomas Becket in medieval England to Archbishop Oscar Romero in twentieth-century Central America.

Restoring Scriptural Liturgical Prayer

To restore the liturgy to its privileged place as the living heart of the church's life, Vatican II refined the shape of its order, permitted its celebration in the vernacular and restored the participatory role of the assembly. While these directives were of some interest to a number of Christians beyond the church, there was one major decision whose repercussions were destined to reach far beyond Roman Catholicism. The *Constitution on the Sacred Liturgy* directed:

> The treasures of the Bible are to be opened up more lavishly so that a richer fare may be provided for the faithful at the table of God's word. In this way a more representative part of the sacred scriptures will be read to the people in the course of a prescribed number of years (51).

After an intensive period of research and consultation involving thousands of experts in scripture, liturgy and pastoral ministry, this 1963 directive became reality in 1969 with the publication in Latin of the *Lectionary for Mass*. Shortly thereafter, the English edition went into use. In place of the Tridentine Missal's one-year table of epistles and gospels, the Sunday liturgy of the word now featured three scripture readings, arranged in a recurring three-year cycle, with a complementary though less extensive weekday arrangement. A modest revision of this Latin lectionary, with a more extensive introduction and some additions and revisions to the 1969 list of readings, was issued in 1981.[1]

An Ecumenical Movement

Here is where the Holy Spirit's surprises, the ecumenical adventure and the remote preparation for *Prayers for Sundays and Seasons* begins! Within less than a year of its publication, the 1969 version of the Roman lectionary attracted the attention of the liturgists and pastors of a number of Christian churches in the United States and Canada that were themselves embarking on the task of liturgical renewal. With remarkable candor (for which Roman Catholics should be grateful and humble), the compilers of the *Book of Common Worship* (Presbyterian Church USA, Cumberland Presbyterian Church) described the evolution of their work:

> Although six years earlier the committee had proposed a new lectionary, it recognized that the lectionary then being completed by the Roman Catholic Church was superior to the lectionary it had prepared. The committee therefore modified the Roman lectionary for use by Presbyterians and included it in the final publication of *The Worshipbook*. Other denominations also made revisions of the Roman lectionary.[2]

They did indeed! Eventually, three Presbyterian Churches in the United States offered an adapted version for use in their new service books. The Disciples of Christ and the United Church of Christ in the USA adopted this version for optional use. Still other adaptations of the Roman lectionary became part of the *Lutheran Book of Worship* (1978) and the Episcopal Church's *Book of Common Prayer* (1979).[3]

More significantly, however, widespread use of these varying lectionaries led to frustration among clergy and laity who were engaged on a grassroots level in the practical, pastoral work of sermon planning and Bible study in an ecumenical context. By 1974, the Consultation on Church Union (COCU) had published a "consensus edition" gleaned from the lectionaries of the various denominations. From 1978 until 1983, a group known as The Consultation on Common Texts (CCT) worked to produce a common lectionary for study, use and critique. Finally in 1992 the *Revised Common Lectionary* made its appearance, the fruit of almost twenty years of experimentation and six years of testing and revision by CCT, which now includes representatives of the Anglican Church of Canada, Christian Church (Disciples of Christ), Christian Reformed Church in North America, Episcopal Church, Evangelical Lutheran Church in America, Evangelical Lutheran Church in Canada, Free Methodist Church in Canada, International Commission on English in the Liturgy (an agency of 26 Roman Catholic national or international conferences of bishops), Lutheran Church

— Missouri Synod, Polish National Catholic Church, Presbyterian Church (USA), Presbyterian Church in Canada, Reformed Church in America, Roman Catholic Church in the United States, Roman Catholic Church in Canada, Unitarian Universalist Christian Fellowship, United Church of Canada, United Church of Christ and the United Methodist Church.

Revising the Prayers

This expanded and ordered proclamation of scripture quickly became a radiant light in which to look at other parts of the liturgy. For instance, a number of Roman Catholics involved in preparing for Sunday liturgy began to realize that Vatican II's vision of scripture inspiring all of the liturgy was an ideal that seemed not to have been realized in some parts of the celebration. The general intercessions, for instance, too often seemed simply a disconnected series of random petitions with little or no connection to the word that had been proclaimed and preached.

In particular, the scriptural grounding mandated by the Council seemed not to have touched the collects or opening prayers of the Sunday liturgy. In the revised Order of Mass, this was the first of the "presidential prayers," those offered by the presider in the name of the assembly and confirmed by the assembly's Amen. This opening prayer thus functioned almost as a keynote text, setting the tone and directing the attention of the assembly toward the imminent proclamation of the word. The fact that there was only a one-year cycle of collects but a three-year cycle of readings underscored this failure to connect with the scriptures. Scholars pointed to the venerable history of these Roman collects, many of which had passed over in translation to the liturgies of the Reformed churches. They were clearly a precious heritage worth preserving and passing on.

Pastors and scholars increasingly began to acknowledge, however, that Vatican II's insight had been a good one, confirmed now by almost a decade of lectionary use: Scripture should indeed inspire these texts, and scripture's language and vocabulary should echo in them.[4] As it turned out, the Roman Catholic Church in Italy had already taken the lead; its second edition of the Roman Missal provided an optional three-year cycle of collects.[5] The forthcoming English-language sacramentary, newly composed by the International Commission on English in the Liturgy (ICEL), will offer a similar option.

As soon as Liturgy Training Publications began to make the Italian prayers available in an English translation, in its annual *Sourcebook for Sundays and Seasons*, it became clear that this was a welcomed development in the eyes of a wide consensus of planners, presiders and pray-ers in the Roman Catholic Church and beyond it![6]

At the same time, many of the churches that had adopted lectionaries for Sunday worship were revising their orders of daily prayer, known variously as the Liturgy of the Hours and the Daily Office. Psalmody and scripture in an ordered form, intended primarily for communal worship, but easily adaptable for personal use, is a style of prayer that has increasingly replaced random Bible reading among Protestants and the use of devotional prayer books by Roman Catholics. Under the influence of the lectionary, even personal prayer is becoming scriptural and liturgical. What better way to prepare for the Lord's Day worship than to read and pray over the scriptural texts we will hear in the assembly? What better way to prolong the Lord's Day grace and to extend its power than to return to that word again and again in quiet personal prayer and meditation?

What's in *Prayers for Sundays and Seasons?*

Liturgy Training Publications' goal in preparing this book is to present a rich resource in a format marked by simplicity and good liturgical sense. A number of features work together toward this end.

Scripture-inspired Collects

Unlike the more abstract opening prayers of the current sacramentary, these collects take their inspiration, and sometimes even their vocabulary, from the readings appointed for the day in the lectionary. The first prayer offered for each Sunday or feast was composed specifically for this publication. The second is usually a new translation of the collect from the Italian sacramentary, although occasionally it, too, may be a new composition. A few were inspired by prayers in the Spanish and Mozarabic sacramentaries, in the *Liturgy of the Hours* and in the *Book of Common Prayer*.

Planners and presiders in non-Roman churches that follow orders of worship based on the classic structure of the Western rite may wish to use these texts to open the worship service, as the collect of the day or the opening prayer. This approach permits the text to set the tone for the liturgy of the word or time of personal prayer. Alternatively, these prayers may well be used to conclude the liturgy of the word, the entire service or one's personal meditation. In this approach, the prayer summarizes the scriptural message and reinforces its comfort and/or challenge to the one who has heard or prayed over the biblical text.

Lectionary References

At the heart of each entry are the references to the scriptures that shape the day's liturgy of the word. In side-by-side columns, the citations from the Roman *Lectionary for Mass*, which is the basis for this publication, and the *Revised Common Lectionary* citations are presented. Not only does the presentation of both lectionary references permit use of *Prayers for Sundays and Seasons* by Christians from different churches, but users from each tradition will be enriched by the insights of the other.

Notice that from Proper 4 to Proper 29 (the Ninth to the Thirty-fourth Sundays in Ordinary Time), the *Revised Common Lectionary* offers two first readings, each of which is paired with a psalm response. This provides for two patterns of First Testament readings. By consistently selecting the first option, the reader will follow a series of semicontinuous readings from various books of the Bible for two or more Sundays. The second option relates closely to the gospel for each Sunday. Those who select readings for congregational use should consistently choose either the first or the second option and use the psalm assigned to the reading chosen.

General Intercessions

In the classic orders of Western liturgy, especially in their revised forms, hearing the word and reflecting on it leads quite naturally to intercessory prayer. The Pastoral Introduction to the Order of Mass, composed for the revision of the sacramentary currently being prepared by ICEL, thus describes this form of prayer:

> Enlightened and moved by God's word, the assembly exercises its priestly function by interceding for

all humanity. Because "the joy and hope, the struggle and anguish of the people of this age and especially of the poor and those suffering in any way are the joy and hope, the struggle and anguish of Christ's disciples,"[7] the church prays not just for its own needs but for the salvation of the world, for civil authorities, for those oppressed by any burden, and for the local community, particularly those who are sick or who have died.[8]

Thus, even though the intercessions may be quite concrete or particular in content, they should always look beyond the concerns of the local assembly to the needs of the whole church and of the wider world. As such, they are a sign of the communion of the particular assembly with all other assemblies and with the universal church[9] (96–97).

Following the general sequence presented here, *Prayers for Sundays and Seasons* presents, for each set of readings, petitions that draw not only their intention but their very vocabulary from the scriptures just proclaimed or prayed over. In this way, the language of prayer echoes the language of proclamation. The goal is to move the hearer, the pray-er, from hearing and interceding to witnessing and doing.

The order of categories presented is that specified in the *General Instruction of the Roman Missal*[10] and spelled out in greater detail in the forthcoming Pastoral Introduction to the Order of Mass.[11]

The Universal Prayer for Good Friday was inspired by and modeled on Monsignor Ronald Knox's *The Holy Week Book* (New York: Sheed and Ward, 1951).

Introduction to the Lord's Prayer

In the words of an old liturgical formula, the Lord's Prayer "gathers all our prayers and petitions together and makes them perfect in the prayer of God's only Son." Varying by season or celebration,[12] an introduction to this unique prayer is provided for each entry.

Invitation to Communion

In addition to the invitation to communion long familiar to the Roman rite ("This is the Lamb of God . . ."), the forthcoming sacramentary provides a second formula adapted from the Byzantine liturgy and the ancient *Bangor Antiphonary* ("God's holy gifts for God's holy people . . .") and a third, adapted from the Lord's "Eucharistic Discourse" in chapter 6 of the Gospel of John and from the Roman Canon ("This is the bread come down from heaven . . . This is the cup of eternal life . . ."). As with the Lord's Prayer, alternate invitations, based on themes of the season or celebration, are provided.

Like the introductions to the Lord's Prayer, these texts may be helpful to presiders at public prayer as a subtle way of linking the liturgy of the word and the liturgy of the eucharist. Those using *Prayers for Sundays and Seasons* for personal prayer may find these brief texts easily memorized as a personal preparation for partaking of holy communion.

Dismissal Texts

According to an age-old custom, the assembly never simply "disperses" or "drifts away" from the liturgy. Rather, the deacon offers an official dismissal to a community now being missioned for witness and service in the world. Indeed, the Latin dismissal, *"Ite, missa est,"* appears to have given the entire eucharistic celebration one of its long enduring names, the Mass. Taking a cue from the variety permitted with the other invitations and introductions, the scriptures of a given season for particular celebration have been mined to provide suggested alternate formularies. For someone leaving a time of personal prayer, this brief text might likewise provide a quiet transition from worship to witness.

A Final Note

Prayers for Sundays and Seasons is not an official liturgical book and is not meant to compete with them; it is meant to be a companion volume and to complement these official resources. The words in *Prayers for Sundays and Seasons* are in some cases ancient words attired in a new translation, scriptural words transformed into intercessory prayer, liturgical texts enshrining the formal sentiments and words of a community baptized, redeemed and sanctified to the service of the living God.

Half a century ago, Dom Gregory Dix said of the eucharist:

> And best of all, week by week and month by month, on a hundred thousand successive Sundays, faithfully, unfailingly, across all the parishes of Christendom, the pastors have done this just to make the *plebs sancta Dei* — the holy common people of God . . . What did the Sunday eucharist in her village church every week for a lifetime mean to the blessed Chione [an otherwise anonymous

fourth-century Christian from Asia Minor] — and to the millions like her then, and every year since? The sheer stupendous quantity of the love of God which this ever repeated action has drawn from the obscure Christian multitudes through the centuries is in itself an overwhelming thought.[13]

The lectionary of Vatican II and the lectionaries it has inspired have already shaped the Sunday worship of a generation of Christians. If the enthusiastic acceptance of the *Revised Common Lectionary* is any indication, Dix's description of the eucharist may be repeated, in a complementary fashion, by the Sunday after Sunday sharing of God's living word. *Prayers for Sundays and Seasons* presents itself to God's people in the Roman Catholic and ecumenical community as a servant of that word.

[1] See *The Liturgy Documents*. Third Edition (Chicago: Liturgy Training Publications, 1991), 117 – 164.

[2] *Book of Common Worship* (Louisville KY: Westminster/John Knox Press, 1993), 5.

[3] See *The Revised Common Lectionary* (Nashville: Abingdon Press, 1992), 75 – 79.

[4] See for instance, Claude Duchesneau, "Une Liturgie Qui Tire Son Inspiration de la Sainte Écriture," *La Maison Dieu* 166 (1986), 119 – 129.

[5] Italian Conference of Bishops, *Messale Romano* (seconda edizione). (Rome: Libreria Editrice Vaticana, 1983), vii.

[6] These texts appeared first in LTP's *Celebrating Liturgy Supplement/Sourcebook 1987* for planners and presiders. They were quickly adopted by the Uniting Church of Australia for their official liturgical books and appear now in those of several Protestant churches.

[7] Vatican Council II, Pastoral Constitution on the Church in the Modern World (*Gaudium et spes*), 7 December 1965, 1.

[8] See *Lectionary for Mass*, 30; see *General Instruction of the Roman Missal*, 45, 46.

[9] ICEL, *The Sacramentary: Segment Three: Order of Mass I* (Washington: ICEL, 1994), 162 – 163.

[10] For the complete text of this document, see the introductory material in any current edition of the sacramentary or in *The Liturgy Documents*, 37 – 104.

[11] Excerpts appear in *Sourcebook for Sundays and Seasons 1997* (Chicago: Liturgy Training Publications, 1996).

[12] See ICEL's Pastoral Introduction to the Order of Mass, 133.

[13] Gregory Dix, *The Shape of the Liturgy* (Westminster: Dacre Press, 1945), 744 – 745.

USING *PRAYERS FOR SUNDAYS AND SEASONS* FOR PUBLIC PRAYER

Planners and presiders will find *Prayers for Sundays and Seasons* an invaluable tool for preparing the Lord's Day liturgy. Here are the resources necessary to bind together the various elements of the liturgy of the word not in an artificially imposed, thematic unity (for the scriptures are so wonderfully rich that any number of themes might be derived from any day's entries) but as a celebration whose every element is shaped by the inspiration and vocabulary of the scriptures.

General Principles

In all elements of which it is fashioned, the assembly's formal liturgical worship demands of those who plan and preside at it certain standards, to which we attend in several ways.

1. Respect for the Multiple Genres of the Community's Prayer

Handed down to us by our forebears are collects, intercessions, introductions, invitations and dismissals. Communal consensus across the ages and historical usage have given some of these a specific structure, a certain tone, a general style and even an approximate length! The official Vatican document that invited us to move beyond the confines of mere translation into the unchartered waters of creativity, nevertheless, wisely quoted Vatican II's *Constitution on the Sacred Liturgy* with its reminder that the ancient texts "transmitted through the tradition of the church [are] the best school and discipline for the creation of new texts so 'that any new forms adopted should in some way grow organically from forms already in existence' (23)" (*Comme le prévoit*: Instruction on the Translation of Liturgical Texts, 43).

2. Reference to Scriptures Proclaimed Throughout the Church

Although, sadly, we Christians are not yet in eucharistic communion, we are already, to a very great extent, in scriptural communion with one another! An unforeseen fruit of Vatican II's liturgical reform, and clearly the work of the Holy Spirit, is the almost universal consensus on a three-year system by which to proclaim and pray over the word of God. While the language of any sincere prayer is, of course, good and acceptable, and any genuine human need a worthy subject of prayer, how much better to draw the themes and the words of our prayer from the very word of God! Vatican II considered it "essential to promote that warm and living love for scripture to which the venerable tradition of both Eastern and Western rites gives testimony" (*Constitution on the Sacred Liturgy*, 24).

3. Ritual, Repetition and Relationship to the Season

With too few fixed texts, there is little opportunity for a seasonal tone to take hold of an assembly and help form its spiritual life during a particular part of the liturgical year. With too many often varied texts, there is likewise scant chance that such a tone will sink in. This resource manual attempts to strike a balance. A fixed text given for a season, part of a season or a block of Sundays within Ordinary Time provides the stability that, by repetition, makes a ritual "sense of the season" more possible. At the same time, the scriptural inspiration, drawn from the readings of the season or Sundays, establishes the particular and unique seasonal tone.

Specific Advice

General Intercessions

While the general intercessions are presented in a ready-to-read format, each community that is truly conscientious about preparing this prayer will want to reserve to itself the option of refining and revising the texts. No one apart from the community, no matter how well intentioned or articulate, can shape the prayers that should well up in the hearts of a particular community.

What is offered here are intentions not only inspired by the day's scriptures but even formulated, as nearly as possible, in their actual vocabulary and language. Their scope is general, as historical research, liturgical scholarship and official directives affirm that these prayers should be, yet there is a balance with concrete images and needs as well, in order to keep the prayer rooted in the reality of human experience.

As noted on page xi, the sequence of categories is that prescribed by the official books of the reformed Roman rite. Under each category, one or more petitions are offered. Those preparing the general intercessions for public worship would, ordinarily, choose only one petition from each category. Morever, each set of intercessions is cast in a consistent style. Within a given set, for instance, each petition begins with "For" or "That." Occasionally, when several petitions are provided under the same category, an intercession in both styles is presented. In preparing the final text for public worship, planners will want to choose or rewrite the petitions so as to maintain a consistency of style. Phrases are balanced for length, style and rhythm. Where rewriting may be necessary or desirable, the text as given can still stand as a model and guideline for original composition. Shorter intercessions may be obtained by reading those that begin with "For" only up to the colon or the first comma.

Scriptural Collects

Each community will likewise need to decide where and when either scriptural collect prayer might appropriately occur. Whichever is chosen to conclude the general intercessions will need to conclude with the short ending (e.g., "We ask this through Jesus Christ our Lord"), as opposed to the full trinitarian formula (e.g., "We ask this through our Lord Jesus Christ, your Son, who lives and reigns with you in the unity of the Holy Spirit, God for ever and ever") that is at the end of each prayer as it is given here.

Introductions, Invitations and Dismissals

With regard to introductions to the Lord's Prayer, invitations to Holy Communion and dismissals, users of *Prayers for Sundays and Seasons* will find here formulae appropriate to the seasonal tone, scriptural in their inspiration, and similar in length, style and rhythm to the models in the sacramentary.

As with everything that Liturgy Training Publications produces, it is the hope of the author and the editors that this book is helpful in the genuine implementation of the spirit of the liturgy renewed by the Second Vatican Council.

USING *PRAYERS FOR SUNDAYS AND SEASONS* FOR PERSONAL PRAYER

Over 30 years ago, Vatican II's *Constitution on the Sacred Liturgy* saw clearly that "in order that the liturgy may possess its full effectiveness, it is necessary that the faithful come to it with proper dispositions, that their minds be attuned to their voices and that they cooperate with divine grace, lest they receive it in vain" (11). The *Constitution* went on to note immediately that "the spiritual life . . . is not limited solely to participation in the liturgy. Christians are indeed called to pray in union with each other, but they must also enter into their chamber to pray to the Father in secret; further, according to the teaching of the apostle, they should pray without ceasing" (12). Not by accident did the following paragraphs urge that "popular devotions" be brought into harmony with the spirit of the liturgy and related specifically to varying parts of the liturgical year.

Lectio Divina

An ancient term for the kind of prayer this book hopes to serve is *lectio divina*, literally, holy reading. The reference is to the slow and steady, patient and prayerful reflection on a given text of scripture. It represents one of the oldest ways of lifting the mind and heart to God or, more accurately, of opening our minds and hearts to let the mind and heart of God permeate our own. Lectio is not scripture study, although the study of scripture can add a rich dimension to it. Lectio is not preparation for the preaching of a homily or the teaching of a religion class, although both of these activities can benefit from it. Still less is lectio a new system of prayer. Our ancestors in the faith have attempted to describe their experiences of lectio, and their remembrances form part of that sacred family heritage that spans

almost two millennia and knits past, present and future together in that mystery within and beyond space and time that we call the church, the communion of saints.

Lectio is principally about relationship. Specifically, it is about deepening the relationship that already exists between God and the human person, formed in God's image. As with all relationships, this one needs a sense of discipline and a sense of humor to maintain it. One can exult in moments of ecstasy and delight, but that same one must also persevere through periods of dryness and routine. In the day-by-day practice of lectio, room for gloom must never overcome a faith that trusts that glimpses of glory are just around the corner. *Prayers for Sundays and Seasons* is a practical handbook for those who want to make the lectionary scriptures the basis of their lectio.

Movements of Lectio

Spiritual writers, with varying emphases, describe several movements that make up lectio. These movements, which are presented below, are not stages. The word *stages* connotes a linear progression, onward and upward, and may even suggest the possibility of being able to control or program such personal prayer with some precision. But *lectio* is a relationship with ups and downs not unlike other relationships. There is movement back and forth, between, among, and sometimes even over, the several stages. Because this movement involves a human heart endowed with freedom, a heart into which the Spirit has been poured, no one ought to succumb to the lure of progress or the shadow of regression. But wherever one may be in the process called lectio, *Prayers for Sundays and Seasons* is designed to be a friend, to lend a helping hand in starting off, to lean on or come back to as needed, and just to be there as a helpful resource, an ongoing inspiration.

First Movement: Preparation

Like all relationships, lectio is a two-way street: There are things we can do so that the Other has room to move. Many people find a fixed time and place helpful. Others consider these luxuries a complete impossibility. Some adorn the space or create a sacred space through the use of icons, candles or incense.

To begin, recall God's presence in the place of prayer and in the sacred text lying open before you. Call on the Spirit of God for the gift of wisdom and insight as you begin to read. The scriptural prayer or collect might be a good way of beginning a personal time of prayer. Together with the choice of the lectionary readings, such a prayer links us to the communion of saints in which all the baptized live and pray.

Second Movement: Lectio, the Reading

With a prayerful heart, read the text until a word or a phrase strikes you, or until God uses a word or phrase to touch your heart, mind, soul. The ancients read their texts aloud. Try it. Read the text aloud, softly to yourself, if this can be done without disturbing others. It may help center any wayward thoughts. Or form the words with your mouth as you read. This simple technique heightens the text's impact, letting the word form as we form the words with our lips.

Third Movement: *Meditatio* or *Ruminatio*

The first Christians who committed to writing their experience with this kind of prayer used the word lectio only for the first movement of their prayer. We move on to *meditatio*, literally softly murmuring, or *ruminatio*, literally "chewing" the text, as a cow chews its cud, extracting whatever God may intend us to obtain from it.

Fourth Movement: *Oratio*

The fruit of *meditatio* is this more formal prayer. With words, or even beyond words, we speak to the God who has spoken to us, or with whom we have been in dialogue through the conversation established by opening and reading the sacred text. Here again, the scripture-inspired prayers may give voice to the thoughts of the heart. Or the intercessions in *Prayers*

for Sundays and Seasons may help move you to intercede for others.

Fifth Movement: *Contemplatio*

Oratio sometimes leads to this glimpse of glory, the quiet peace, burning fire, rushing floods or sweet assurance of which the mystics speak, or at least try. The images are contradictory because the experience is ineffable, beyond words, defying accurate description. So "here let me rest from my high fantasy," as Dante says on entering his time of *contemplatio*.

Sixth Movement: Harvest

When the time of prayer is over, or the movement of prayer has ceased, there comes a natural moment in which to harvest the fruit of the lectio sowing. Like the monastic Christians, you might take from lectio a sentence, a phrase, even a word to use throughout the day, as a way of refocusing a wandering heart or of directing prayers to the presence of God. If you wish to close out the period of quiet reflection with a slow and prayerful offering of the Lord's Prayer, *Prayers for Sundays and Seasons* provides a scripturally and seasonally oriented introduction. If you are leaving the time of lectio to celebrate the eucharist, the invitation to holy communion in *Prayers for Sundays and Seasons* may be helpful.

Thus, what *Prayers for Sundays and Seasons* very much hopes to be is not merely another resource for those serving the assembly in roles of planning and presiding but a personal manual of liturgical prayer for those "in their chambers praying in secret," — but nevertheless exercising their baptismal priesthood in that time of reading, contemplation and intercession — and preparing at the same time to exercise that same baptismal priesthood publically, as members of the Lord's Day eucharistic assembly.

FIRST SUNDAY OF ADVENT

God our maker,
whose name is "our Redeemer from of old":
Tear open the heavens and come down!

Keep us faithful to building your kingdom,
alert to your presence in those around us,
and blameless in our witness
until the dawning of the day of our Lord Jesus Christ,
who was, who is and who is to come,
your Son who lives and reigns with you
in the unity of the Holy Spirit,
God for ever and ever.

Through all generations, O God,
your faithfulness endures,
and your fidelity to the covenant can never fail.
Since you are the potter and we the work of your
    hands,
remember us and strengthen us to the end by your
    grace;
that, with a love beyond reproach,
we may faithfully keep watch
for the glorious coming of our Redeemer,
and be found blameless
on the day of your Son, our Lord Jesus Christ,
who lives and reigns with you
in the unity of the Holy Spirit,
God for ever and ever.

Roman Lectionary	**Revised Common Lectionary**
Isaiah 63:16b –17, 19b; 64:2b – 7	Isaiah 64:1– 9
Psalm 80:2 – 3, 15 –16, 18 –19	Psalm 80:1– 7, 17–19
1 Corinthians 1:3 – 9	1 Corinthians 1:3 – 9
Mark 13:33 – 37	Mark 13:24 – 37

General Intercessions

Let us call upon the name of God,
who faithfully acts on behalf of those who wait in hope.

FOR THE CHURCH
That the church may be fully engaged in the task Christ has entrusted to it
and be found awake and alert for the coming of the Lord.

FOR THE WORLD
That the leaders of nations may turn their hands from violence and iniquity
and embrace instead the ways of righteousness and peace.

FOR THOSE OPPRESSED, AFFLICTED OR IN NEED
That hardened hearts may be softened and straying steps guided home
by the touch of God's hand and the love of Christians.

FOR THE NEEDS OF THE LOCAL COMMUNITY

That the sick (especially N.) may be supported by the presence and prayers of family and friends, and so experience the healing power of our Redeemer.

FOR THE CHRISTIAN ASSEMBLY

That this assembly may be shaped by God's hand, enriched by God's gifts, and strengthened to be blameless on the day of our Lord Jesus Christ.

FOR THE DEAD

That the departed (especially N.) may rejoice as they are called into fellowship with Christ by the God who is faithful.

Introduction to the Lord's Prayer

Let us pray for the coming of the kingdom as Jesus taught us:

Invitation to Holy Communion

Behold the Lord whose advent we await, who will come with glory on the day of judgment. Blessed are those who are called to the banquet of the Lamb.

Dismissal

Go forth in peace to prepare the way of the Lord.

◆

SECOND SUNDAY OF ADVENT

O God,
whose word is comfort
and whose promise is a new creation,
prepare the way in the wilderness of our world.

Open our eyes to the One who comes into our midst,
that by lives of holiness and service
we may hasten the coming of that day
and be found at peace when at last it dawns.

We ask this through our Lord Jesus Christ,
who was, who is and who is to come,
your Son who lives and reigns with you
in the unity of the Holy Spirit,
God for ever and ever.

O God of all consolation,
to us who journey as pilgrims through time
you have promised new heavens and a new earth.
Speak today to the inmost heart of your people,
that, leading lives of holiness and godliness,
and with a faith free from spot or blemish,
we may hasten toward that day
on which you will manifest
in the fullness of its splendor
the glory of your holy name.

We ask this through our Lord Jesus Christ, your Son,
who lives and reigns with you
in the unity of the Holy Spirit,
God for ever and ever.

Roman Lectionary
Isaiah 40:1– 5, 9 –11
Psalm 85:9 – 14
2 Peter 3:8 –14
Mark 1:1– 8

Revised Common Lectionary
Isaiah 40:1–11
Psalm 85:1– 2, 8 –13
2 Peter 3:8 –15a
Mark 1:1– 8

General Intercessions

As we await the fulfillment of God's promise,
let us offer prayer to the Lord whose patience is our salvation.

> FOR THE CHURCH
> For the church, that it may herald the glad tidings of God's coming
> to gather and comfort all people.

> FOR THE WORLD
> For the world, that its striving for peace may foreshadow
> the new heavens and new earth where righteousness will be at home.

For the oppressed, that worldly pride may be brought low, the downtrodden lifted up,
and the uneven ground leveled to become a highway for God's justice.

FOR THE NEEDS OF THE LOCAL COMMUNITY
For the catechumens (in this parish and) throughout the church, that,
led by the Good Shepherd, they may come to baptism and new life in the Holy Spirit.

For the sick and homebound (especially N.), that, through our ministry of care and communion,
God may speak tenderly to them with a comfort that banishes fear.

FOR THE CHRISTIAN ASSEMBLY
For this eucharistic assembly, that, by leading lives of holiness and godliness,
we may wait for the day of God and hasten its coming.

FOR THE DEAD
For those gone before us (especially N.), that, found at peace, without spot or blemish,
they may receive from the Lord's hand the reward and recompense of life.

Introduction to the Lord's Prayer

Let us pray for the coming of the kingdom as Jesus taught us:

Invitation to Holy Communion

Behold the Lord whose advent we await, who will come with glory on the day of judgment.
Blessed are those who are called to the banquet of the Lamb.

Dismissal

Go forth in peace to prepare the way of the Lord.

THIRD SUNDAY OF ADVENT

God of peace,
whose word is good news to the oppressed,
healing for the brokenhearted
and freedom for all who are held bound,
gladden our hearts and fashion the earth
into a garden of righteousness and praise!

Sanctify us entirely, in spirit, soul and body,
for the coming of the One
who even now is among us,
your Son, our Lord Jesus Christ,
who was, who is and who is to come,
your Son, who lives and reigns with you
in the unity of the Holy Spirit,
God for ever and ever.

O God, protector of the oppressed,
healer of the brokenhearted,
you invite all people to share the joy and peace
    of your reign.
Show us your loving kindness.
Sanctify our hearts, and keep them blameless
that we may generously prepare the way
for the Savior who is coming:
your Son, our Lord Jesus Christ,
who lives and reigns with you
in the unity of the Holy Spirit,
God for ever and ever.

Roman Lectionary
Isaiah 61:1– 2a, 10 –11
Luke 1:46 – 50, 53 – 54
1 Thessalonians 5:16 – 24
John 1:6 – 8, 19 – 28

Revised Common Lectionary
Isaiah 61:1– 4, 8 –11
Psalm 126
or
Luke 1:47– 55
1 Thessalonians 5:16 – 24
John 1:6 – 8, 19 – 28

General Intercessions

To the God of peace, let us pray without ceasing, rejoicing always in the One who calls us,
the God who is faithful.

FOR THE CHURCH
That all the baptized, anointed by the Spirit,
may proclaim the good news of this year of the Lord's favor.

FOR THE WORLD
That the Lord God may cause righteousness and praise
to spring up as a garden of peace for all nations.

FOR THOSE OPPRESSED, AFFLICTED OR IN NEED
That those held captive by disease or addiction, by prejudice or oppression,
may be released to rejoice in the liberty of God's children.

That we may recognize the One who stands among us in the brokenhearted
and gladly serve Christ by binding up their wounds.

That those who suffer in body, mind or spirit (especially N.)
may be made sound and whole again.

That we may hold fast to what is good, abstain from every form of evil
and be sanctified entirely for the coming of our Lord Jesus Christ.

That the faithful departed (especially N.)
may be clothed with the garment of salvation at the banquet of the Lamb.

Introduction to the Lord's Prayer

Before December 17
Let us pray for the coming of the kingdom as Jesus taught us:

After December 17
Patiently awaiting the Lord whose coming is near,
let us rejoice as we lift up our hands and pray:

Invitation to Holy Communion

Before December 17
Behold the Lord whose advent we await, who will come with glory on the day of judgment.
Blessed are those who are called to the banquet of the Lamb.

After December 17
Behold the One who comes to gather God's people and to feed the Lord's flock.
Blessed are those who are called to the banquet of the Lamb.

Dismissal

Before December 17
Go forth in peace to prepare the way of the Lord.

After December 17
The Lord's coming is close at hand.
Go forth in peace to prepare the way of the Lord.

FOURTH SUNDAY OF ADVENT

Eternal God, whom the heavens cannot contain,
you have chosen as your tabernacle
the womb of Mary, the Virgin of Nazareth.

Overshadow us with your power,
form us as your daughters and sons
and knit us together as your holy people
according to your word.

For you nothing is impossible,
and so we offer you our prayer
through our Lord Jesus Christ,
who was, who is and who is to come,
your Son, who lives and reigns with you
in the unity of the Holy Spirit,
God for ever and ever.

Great and merciful God,
from among this world's lowly and humble
you choose your servants
and call them to work with you
to fulfill your loving plan of salvation.
By the power of your Spirit,
make your church fertile and fruitful,
that, imitating the obedient faith of Mary,
the church may welcome your word of life
and so become the joyful mother
    of countless offspring,
a great and holy posterity of children
    destined for undying life.

We ask this through our Lord Jesus Christ, your Son,
who lives and reigns with you
in the unity of the Holy Spirit,
God for ever and ever.

Roman Lectionary
2 Samuel 7:1–5, 8b–12, 14a, 16
Psalm 89:2–5, 27, 29
Romans 16:25–27
Luke 1:26–38

Revised Common Lectionary
2 Samuel 7:1–11, 16
Luke 1:47–55
or
Psalm 89:1–4, 19–26
Romans 16:25–27
Luke 1:26–38

General Intercessions

Let us bring the needs of all to the Rock of our salvation, whose steadfast love endures forever.

FOR THE CHURCH
For the people of God, the house the Lord is building:
May all who call on God's name grow in the obedience of faith.

FOR THE WORLD
For all the peoples of earth, one kingdom of God:
May all who love peace be sheltered from violence.

For those in doubt or fear, perplexed by life's mystery:
May their anxiety yield to trust in God's saving plan and purpose.

FOR THE NEEDS OF THE LOCAL COMMUNITY
For those parents (in our community) awaiting the birth of a child:
Like the Virgin Mary may they joyfully ponder God's power and goodness.

For the homeless and destitute, those abandoned by society:
May God bring them to their own place and surround them with loving care.

FOR THE CHRISTIAN ASSEMBLY
For this assembly and its life of worship and witness:
May the Spirit come upon us, the power of the Most High overshadow us.

FOR THE DEAD
For those whose days are fulfilled and who are gathered with our ancestors (especially N.):
May they be established in God's kingdom of peace and rest.

Introduction to the Lord's Prayer

Patiently awaiting the Lord whose coming is near,
let us rejoice as we lift up our hands and pray:

Invitation to Holy Communion

Behold the One who comes to gather God's people and to feed the Lord's flock.
Blessed are those who are called to the banquet of the Lamb.

Dismissal

The Lord's coming is close at hand.
Go forth in peace to prepare the way of the Lord.

THE BIRTH OF THE LORD

VIGIL

Abiding with you forever in glory, O God,
your only-begotten child is born among us in time.

May we ever welcome your Son
to the warmth of an earthly home
and so open for all earth's children
a path that leads us home.

We ask this through our Lord Jesus Christ, your Son,
who lives and reigns with you
in the unity of the Holy Spirit,
God for ever and ever.

Shaped by your hand, O God of all the generations,
we are a crown of beauty, a royal diadem,
a land you marry and a people in whom you delight!

With Sarah and Tamar, with Rahab and Ruth,
with all of our ancestors, sinners and saints,
from Abraham and David to Joseph and Mary,
we praise your steadfast love and sing your faithful
    covenant.
Make us a people firm to trust in your promises
and quick to do your will.

We ask this through our Lord Jesus Christ,
Emmanuel, God with us,
your Son who lives and reigns with you
in the unity of the Holy Spirit,
God for ever and ever.

Roman Lectionary

Isaiah 62:1–5
Psalm 89:4–5, 16–17, 27, 29
Acts 13:16–17, 22–25
Matthew 1:1–25 or 1:18–25

Revised Common Lectionary

Any of the following Christmas Propers may be used on Christmas Eve/Day.

PROPER I: Isaiah 9:2–7
       Psalm 96
       Titus 2:11–14
       Luke 2:1–14, (15–20)

PROPER II: Isaiah 62:6–12
       Psalm 97
       Titus 3:4–7
       Luke 2:(1–7), 8–20

PROPER III: Isaiah 52:7–10
       Psalm 98
       Hebrews 1:1–4, (5–12)
       John 1:1–14

General Intercessions

With confidence and joy, let us pray to the God
who delights and rejoices in the children of earth.

FOR THE CHURCH
For the church throughout the world, that, shining as a crown of beauty in the hand of the Lord,
it may herald for all peoples the dawn of God's saving love.

FOR THE WORLD
For lands made desolate by war,
that the Savior's birth may signal the marriage of heaven and earth,
the rebuilding of justice and peace.

FOR THOSE OPPRESSED, AFFLICTED OR IN NEED
For those who feel forsaken or abandoned,
that Christians may offer the loving care and concern that bears witness to God's abiding
presence with them.

FOR THE NEEDS OF THE LOCAL COMMUNITY
For catechumens (in our parish and) throughout the church,
that the community's Christmas joy may intensify their desire to meet the One
who is coming in baptism to be their Savior.

FOR THE CHRISTIAN ASSEMBLY
For this community, that, by our love for one another and our outreach to the unloved,
we may proclaim that God is Emmanuel, God-is-with-us.

FOR THE DEAD
For those gone before us in death (especially N.),
that they may rejoice in the presence of Mary's child, Jesus, who saves the people from their sins.

Introduction to the Lord's Prayer

The Word became flesh and dwelled among us, that as children of God we might dare to pray:

Invitation to Holy Communion

Behold Mary's child, the promised Savior, of whose fullness we have all received.
Blessed are those who are called to the banquet of the Lamb.

Dismissal

Rejoicing in Emmanuel, God-is-with-us, go in peace to love and serve the Lord.

25
DECEMBER
THE BIRTH OF THE LORD
DURING THE NIGHT

While all the world, Lord God,
lay wrapped in deepest silence,
and night had reached its midpoint,
your all-powerful Word came down.

As year by year the beauty of this night returns,
growing old with the aged
and renewed in the wonder of children,
so may we, grown old in sin but reborn to grace,
proclaim with our lives what we chant with our lips:
Glory to you, our God, in the highest heaven,
peace on earth and in the depths of every heart.

We ask this through our Lord Jesus Christ, your Son,
who lives and reigns with you
in the unity of the Holy Spirit,
God for ever and ever.

God of midnight's (nighttime's) deepest silence
and heaven's brightest glory,
whose radiant majesty angelic choirs praise
and whose hidden glory lowly shepherds adore,
your grace has appeared, bringing salvation to all,
in a child wrapped in swaddling clothes and lying
    in a manger.

Upon the deep darkness of our world
shine the light of your countenance
that our hearts may exult and sing for joy
    at the savior's coming,
with angels and shepherds, with Mary and Joseph,
and with all people of good will
    who long for your peace.

We ask this through our Lord Jesus Christ,
Emmanuel, God with us,
your Son who lives and reigns with you
in the unity of the Holy Spirit,
God for ever and ever.

Roman Lectionary
Isaiah 9:1–6
Psalm 96:1–3, 11–13
Titus 2:11–14
Luke 2:1–14

Revised Common Lectionary
Any of the following Christmas Propers may be used on Christmas Eve or Day.

PROPER I: Isaiah 9:2–7
Psalm 96
Titus 2:11–14
Luke 2:1–14, (15–20)

PROPER II: Isaiah 62:6–12
Psalm 97
Titus 3:4–7
Luke 2:(1–7), 8–20

PROPER III: Isaiah 52:7–10
Psalm 98
Hebrews 1:1–4, (5–12)
John 1:1–14

General Intercessions

Celebrating the birth that brings grace and salvation to all,
let us place before God our needs and those of the whole world.

FOR THE CHURCH

For the church here and throughout the world, that our worship and praise may give glory to God,
and our witness and ministry promote peace on earth.

FOR THE WORLD

For peoples of every race and nation, that the celebration of the birth of the Prince of Peace
may encourage a new birth of righteousness and justice.

FOR THOSE OPPRESSED, AFFLICTED OR IN NEED

For those bowed down by injustice or despair, that the power of God and the zeal of God's servants
may break the rod of oppression and lift the yoke of life's burdens.

For refugees and aliens, for homeless people and unwed mothers, that in them we may see
the image of Mary and Joseph, and recognize the face of Christ.

FOR THE NEEDS OF THE LOCAL COMMUNITY

For family and friends near and far, for the hospitalized and homebound,
that the good news of Christmas may be for all who are dear to us the end of darkness and fear,
the dawn of light and joy.

FOR THE CHRISTIAN ASSEMBLY

For this eucharistic assembly, that by the grace of Christ's coming we may live upright and godly lives,
and bear witness to our blessed hope for the Savior's glorious return.

FOR THE DEAD

For those who have died in Christ (especially N.),
that the Savior whose appearing they longed for may gladden them with the vision of heaven's glory.

Introduction to the Lord's Prayer

The Word became flesh and dwelled among us,
that as children of God we might dare to pray:

Invitation to Holy Communion

Behold Mary's child, the promised Savior, of whose fullness we have all received.
Blessed are those who are called to the banquet of the Lamb.

Dismissal

Rejoicing in Emmanuel, God-is-with-us, go in peace to love and serve the Lord.

THE BIRTH OF THE LORD

AT DAWN

The Sun of Justice has dawned upon us, O God,
with healing in his wings,
and we, so often full of fear,
rejoice to hear your prophet call us "the holy people,"
"redeemed," "sought out," "a city not forsaken."

As your Son, in putting on our flesh,
chose to become our partner in weakness,
so may we, through the water of rebirth
and renewal by the Holy Spirit,
become partners with your Son
in the new life announced this morning,
the gospel we ponder in our hearts.

We ask this through our Lord Jesus Christ, your Son,
who lives and reigns with you
in the unity of the Holy Spirit,
God for ever and ever.

In this most gentle dawn,
O good and most gracious God,
we have hastened to behold the wonder that has
    taken place,
for the goodness and loving kindness of our Savior
    has appeared.

Give us words inspired enough to make known
the mercy that has touched our lives,
deeds loving enough to bear witness
to the treasure you have bestowed,
and hearts simple enough to ponder
the mystery of your gracious and abiding love.

We ask this through our Lord Jesus Christ,
Emmanuel, God with us,
your Son who lives and reigns with you
in the unity of the Holy Spirit,
God for ever and ever.

Roman Lectionary

Isaiah 62:11–12
Psalm 97: 1, 6, 11–12
Titus 3:4 – 7
Luke 2:15 – 20

Revised Common Lectionary

*Any of the following Christmas Propers may be used on
Christmas Eve or Day.*

PROPER I: Isaiah 9:2 – 7
      Psalm 96
      Titus 2:11–14
      Luke 2:1–14, (15 – 20)

PROPER II: Isaiah 62:6 –12
      Psalm 97
      Titus 3:4 – 7
      Luke 2:(1– 7), 8 – 20

PROPER III: Isaiah 52:7–10
      Psalm 98
      Hebrews 1:1– 4, (5 –12)
      John 1:1–14

General Intercessions

Let us offer our petitions to God our Savior,
whose goodness and loving kindness have dawned on us.

FOR THE CHURCH

For God's holy people, the redeemed of the Lord,
that believers may draw many to share the inheritance of hope in eternal life.

FOR THE WORLD

For our nation and for all peoples to the end of the earth,
that the world may be a city not forsaken but sought out for God's peace.

FOR THOSE OPPRESSED, AFFLICTED OR IN NEED

For those marginalized and scorned by society,
that like the shepherds of old they may hear from God's messengers the good news of Christ's love.

For the lowly and powerless of this world,
that they may hear the good news that they, before all others, are welcome at the manger of Christ.

FOR THE NEEDS OF THE LOCAL COMMUNITY

For catechumens (here and) everywhere in the church,
that they may be strengthened by the joyful witness of those already baptized in the water of rebirth.

FOR THE CHRISTIAN ASSEMBLY

For all of us gathered at this Christmas feast,
that, like Mary, we may ponder God's word in our hearts and bring forth Christ into the world.

FOR THE DEAD

For the faithful departed (especially N.),
that, justified by Christ's mercy and grace, they may glorify and praise God for all eternity.

Introduction to the Lord's Prayer

The Word became flesh and dwelled among us,
that as children of God we might dare to pray:

Invitation to Holy Communion

Behold Mary's child, the promised Savior, of whose fullness we have all received.
Blessed are those who are called to the banquet of the Lamb.

Dismissal

Rejoicing in Emmanuel, God-is-with-us, go in peace to love and serve the Lord.

25
DECEMBER
THE BIRTH OF THE LORD
DURING THE DAY

Your Word, O God of ageless glory,
dwelling with you from before time,
has become flesh and lived among us,
and we have seen the glory of your Christ.

Place on our lips the word of salvation,
in our hearts a love that welcomes all,
and, in the depths of our being,
the light of faith and hope,
which the darkness can never overcome.

We ask this through our Lord Jesus Christ, your Son,
who lives and reigns with you
in the unity of the Holy Spirit,
God for ever and ever.

In the beginning, O God, was your Word,
and now in time your Word becomes flesh,
the light that shines unconquered
through the darkness of the ages
and has made his dwelling place among us
transforming earth's gloom into heaven's glory.

As we behold upon the mountains
the messenger who announces your peace,
touch our lips as well that we may lift up our voices
as bearers of good news and heralds of salvation.

We ask this through our Lord Jesus Christ,
Emmanuel, God with us,
your Son who lives and reigns with you
in the unity of the Holy Spirit,
God for ever and ever.

Roman Lectionary
Isaiah 52:7–10
Psalm 98:1–6
Hebrews 1:1–6
John 1:1–18 *or* 1:1–5, 9–14

Revised Common Lectionary
Any of the following Christmas Propers may be used on Christmas Eve or Day.

PROPER I: Isaiah 9:2–7
Psalm 96
Titus 2:11–14
Luke 2:1–14, (15–20)

PROPER II: Isaiah 62:6–12
Psalm 97
Titus 3:4–7
Luke 2:(1–7), 8–20

PROPER III: Isaiah 52:7–10
Psalm 98
Hebrews 1:1–4, (5–12)
John 1:1–14

General Intercessions

As Christmas fills the earth with the good news of the Word made flesh,
let our prayer embrace the needs of all God's children.

FOR THE CHURCH
For the church's worldwide ministry of compassion,
that by these works of charity we may serve the God incarnate among us.

FOR THE WORLD
For international efforts toward mutual understanding,
that all nations may gladly welcome messengers who announce peace.

FOR THOSE OPPRESSED, AFFLICTED OR IN NEED
For the homeless and the unemployed, for the lonely and bereaved,
for all who find the winter season difficult or the holidays a burden,
that Christians may be for them the instruments of Christ's light and life.

FOR THE NEEDS OF THE LOCAL COMMUNITY
For families reunited by the holidays, for homes gladdened by children,
and for hearts made joyful by friendship,
that all may bless the God who comforts and sustains us with these gifts.

FOR THE CHRISTIAN ASSEMBLY
For all of us, friends and strangers, one community gathered here,
that we may come to see and cherish each other in the light of Christ.

FOR THE DEAD
For our beloved departed who accepted and believed in Christ (especially N.),
that they may see Christ now in the fullness of the Father's glory.

Introduction to the Lord's Prayer

The Word became flesh and dwelled among us, that as children of God we might dare to pray:

Invitation to Holy Communion

Behold Mary's child, the promised Savior, of whose fullness we have all received.
Blessed are those who are called to the banquet of the Lamb.

Dismissal

Rejoicing in Emmanuel, God-is-with-us, go in peace to love and serve the Lord.

THE HOLY FAMILY
SUNDAY AFTER CHRISTMAS DAY

O God, Creator all-powerful,
in your wisdom and love,
your Son, begotten before the dawn of time,
became in time a member of our human family.

Give to parents the life-giving fruitfulness
of your own divine love.
To daughters and sons give wisdom, godliness
    and grace.
Make us all grow as your own Son did
    within the holy family
to the praise and glory of your name.

We ask this through our Lord Jesus Christ, your Son,
who lives and reigns with you
in the unity of the Holy Spirit,
God for ever and ever.

God of the covenant,
looking graciously upon their faith,
you brought Abraham joy and Sarah laughter
in the birth of their child
and in the beginnings of a family countless
    as the stars of heaven.
With Simeon and Anna, with Mary and Joseph,
our eyes have seen your salvation,
and we hold it in our hands.

Strengthen us to embrace your sign of contradiction,
fill us with the wisdom to trust in your promises,
and let your gracious favor rest on this family
    you have gathered.

We ask this through our Lord Jesus Christ,
Emmanuel, God with us,
your Son who lives and reigns with you
in the unity of the Holy Spirit,
God for ever and ever.

Roman Lectionary
Genesis 15:1–6; 21:1–3 *or* Sirach 3:2–6, 12–14
Psalm 128:1–5
Hebrews 11:8, 11–12, 17–19 *or* Colossians 3:12–17, (18–21)
Luke 2:22–40 *or* 39–40

Revised Common Lectionary
Isaiah 61:10 — 62:3
Psalm 148
Galatians 4:4–7
Luke 2:22–40

General Intercessions

Guided by the Spirit and gathered in the temple of the Lord,
let us pray for all the peoples of earth with whom we form one family.

FOR THE CHURCH
That, like Abraham and Sarah, the family of the church may go wherever God calls it,
fearing nothing and filled with faith.

FOR THE WORLD
That the multitude of nations may quickly discover their common destiny,
the inheritance of peace and the covenant of God's love.

FOR THOSE OPPRESSED, AFFLICTED OR IN NEED
That migrants and refugees, the poor and the lowly may be reverenced
as those in whom and through whom God chooses to come among us.

FOR THE NEEDS OF THE LOCAL COMMUNITY
That we may cherish our senior citizens who, like Simeon and Anna,
enrich this community with their faithful prayer and dedicated service.

That God may bless our families with the joy of love and laughter,
strength in time of testing and faith in God's plan for the future.

FOR THE CHRISTIAN ASSEMBLY
That, gathered as one family at the table of word and eucharist,
we may welcome Christ as a light of revelation and God's promise fulfilled.

FOR THE DEAD
That our family members who have died in Christ (especially N.)
may see the salvation God has prepared for those who trust.

Introduction to the Lord's Prayer

The Word became flesh and dwelled among us,
that as children of God we might dare to pray:

Invitation to Holy Communion

Behold Mary's child, the promised Savior, of whose fullness we have all received.
Blessed are those who are called to the banquet of the Lamb.

Dismissal

Rejoicing in Emmanuel, God-is-with-us, go in peace to love and serve the Lord.

1
JANUARY
MARY, MOTHER OF GOD
HOLY NAME OF JESUS

God of peace,
whose providence guides the changing seasons
of every year and of all our lives:
in the fullness of time,
you fashioned in the Virgin Mother Mary
a dwelling place for your Word made flesh among us.

Bless with the joy of your Holy Spirit,
the first day of this new year,
that through all the days allotted to us,
we may, like Mary,
rejoice in grace and embrace your will.

We ask this through our Lord Jesus Christ, your Son,
who lives and reigns with you
in the unity of the Holy Spirit,
God for ever and ever.

O God, the Maker of each year's dawning,
the Guardian of its unfolding days,
and the Crown of its appointed end:
yours is the Name invoked upon us,
yours the Son born to us of a woman,
yours the Spirit poured forth into our hearts.

Bless and keep, in this new year,
all who cry out to you, "Abba!"
Make your face to shine on all whom you have
adopted in Mary's Son.
Lift up your countenance,
and in the power of your Spirit,
give us peace.

We ask this through our Lord Jesus Christ,
Emmanuel, God with us,
your Son who lives and reigns with you
in the unity of the Holy Spirit,
God for ever and ever.

Roman Lectionary
Numbers 6:22–27
Psalm 67:2–3, 5–6, 8
Galatians 4:4–7
Luke 2:16–21

Revised Common Lectionary
HOLY NAME OF JESUS/MARY, MOTHER OF GOD
 Numbers 6:22–27
 Psalm 8
 Galatians 4:4–7 *or* Philippians 2:5–13
 Luke 2:15–21
NEW YEAR'S DAY
 Ecclesiastes 3:1–13
 Psalm 8
 Revelation 21:1–6a
 Matthew 25:31–46

General Intercessions

Glorifying and praising God for the good news we have heard and seen,
let us offer intercession through the Son born of the Virgin Mother.

FOR THE CHURCH
For God's holy church:
May it champion humankind's struggle for freedom from every slavery.

FOR THE WORLD
For leaders of nations:
May they dedicate this New Year to a more intensive search for peace.

FOR THOSE OPPRESSED, AFFLICTED OR IN NEED
For those who seek a deeper meaning to their lives:
May they find in Christ a teacher to follow and a purpose to live for.

FOR THE NEEDS OF THE LOCAL COMMUNITY
For those who will face new beginnings in the year ahead:
May their courage and confidence be in God, whose face shines on them.

FOR THE CHRISTIAN ASSEMBLY
For all of us who begin this New Year at the table of God's word (and the Lord's Supper):
May we draw daily strength from calling on God in prayer.

FOR THE DEAD
For all who were named as God's own in this life (especially N.):
May the Lord lift up his countenance on them now and give them peace.

Introduction to the Lord's Prayer

The Word became flesh and dwelled among us,
that as children of God we might dare to pray:

Invitation to Holy Communion

Behold Mary's child, the promised Savior, of whose fullness we have all received.
Blessed are those who are called to the banquet of the Lamb.

Dismissal

Rejoicing in Emmanuel, God-is-with-us, go in peace to love and serve the Lord.

SECOND SUNDAY AFTER CHRISTMAS

God of everlasting glory,
you have chosen us and loved us
from before the creation of the world;
and in this Christ, who is Wisdom incarnate,
you have come to dwell in our very midst.

May we welcome this mystery of your love
and thus delight in the joy that will be ours
as children and heirs of your kingdom.

We ask this through our Lord Jesus Christ, your Son,
who lives and reigns with you
in the unity of the Holy Spirit,
God for ever and ever.

Creator God,
whose Word was present with you in the beginning
and whose Wisdom placed herself at the service
    of your plan:

Enlighten us to know the glorious hope to which
    you have called us;
fill us with faith in Jesus and with love toward
    all your people
that we who have seen in Christ the glory
    of your Word made flesh
may bear into the world you so love
the Light no darkness can extinguish:
your Son, our Lord Jesus Christ,
who lives and reigns with you
in the unity of the Holy Spirit,
God for ever and ever.

Roman Lectionary	**Revised Common Lectionary**
Sirach 24:1–4, 8–12	1 Samuel 3:1–10, (11–20)
Psalm 147:12–15, 19–20	Psalm 139:1–6, 13–18
Ephesians 1:3–6, 15–18	1 Corinthians 6:12–20
John 1:1–18 *or* 1:1–5, 9–14	John 1:43–51

General Intercessions

Gathered at prayer in the temple of the Lord,
let us offer our intercession to the God who has called us by name.

FOR THE CHURCH
That the church may listen attentively to the voice of the Lord
and respond with courage and resourcefulness in God's service.

That Pope N., called to exercise the ministry of Peter in God's church,
may inspire by his own example our eager and ready response to Christ.

FOR THE WORLD
That the leaders of nations may hear in the voices of their people
God's own voice summoning the world to a future of justice and peace.

That those who are seeking meaning and purpose for their lives
may come and see in Christ the teacher for whom they search.

FOR THE NEEDS OF THE LOCAL COMMUNITY
That the married couples of our community
may be blessed by God with deepening love and steadfast fidelity.

That educators may inspire our young people to embrace the beauty of chastity
and develop relationships marked by mutual respect.

That (our) catechumens who have come to acknowledge Jesus as Messiah
may stay with us as we learn together from this anointed Teacher.

That we who have heard the good news and followed Jesus
may find others in search of truth and bring them to Jesus.

FOR THE CHRISTIAN ASSEMBLY
That those whom God has called to eternal life (especially N.)
may rejoice to remain forever with the Teacher they followed on earth.

Introduction to the Lord's Prayer

Taught by our Savior's command and formed by the word of God,
we dare to pray:

Invitation to Holy Communion

Behold the Lamb of God, who takes away the sin of the world.
Blessed are those who are called to the banquet of the Lamb.

Dismissal

Listening for God's voice and eager to do God's will, go in peace to love and serve the Lord.

EPIPHANY OF THE LORD

By the light of a star, O God of the universe,
you guided the nations to the Light of the world.

Until this Redeemer comes again in glory,
we, with the Magi, seek the face of the Savior.
Summon us with all those who thirst now
    to the banquet of love.
May our hunger be filled and our thirst be quenched
    with your word of truth.

We ask this through our Lord Jesus Christ, your Son,
who lives and reigns with you
in the unity of the Holy Spirit,
God for ever and ever.

With a star's radiance, O God, you guided the
    nations to the Light;
in a prophet's words you revealed the mystery of the
    Messiah's coming;
through the Magi's gifts you unfolded the richness of
    the Savior's mission.

Scatter again the darkness that covers the earth and
    divides the peoples.
Make our hearts thrill anew to see the multitudes
    carried as sons and daughters in your arms.
In Christ and through Christ's gospel draw the ends
    of the earth into your family,
that disparate cultures and warring nations may be
    gathered together as one.

We ask this through our Lord Jesus Christ,
Emmanuel, God with us,
your Son who lives and reigns with you
in the unity of the Holy Spirit,
God for ever and ever.

Roman Lectionary	**Revised Common Lectionary**
Isaiah 60:1– 6	Isaiah 60:1– 6
Psalm 72:1– 2, 7– 8, 10 –13	Psalm 72:1– 7, 10 –14
Ephesians 3:2 – 3a, 5 – 6	Ephesians 3:1–12
Matthew 2:1–12	Matthew 2:1–12

General Intercessions

Let us intercede for our needs and those of all nations,
upon whom the glory of God has shone in Christ.

FOR THE CHURCH
    For God's holy church, that its light may beckon a rich diversity of peoples
    to come and be heirs with us, members of the one body of Christ.

For nations covered by the clouds of ethnic and racial hatred,
that in this new year their hearts may rejoice at the dawn of peace
and the flourishing of righteousness.

FOR THOSE OPPRESSED, AFFLICTED OR IN NEED
For children abused or neglected, and parents in difficulty or danger,
that the Christian community may offer gifts of care and advocacy, intervention and support.

FOR THE NEEDS OF THE LOCAL COMMUNITY
For all who earnestly seek the face of God,
that this community's faith, hope and love may guide them to the revelation of God's grace.

For (our) catechumens and those seeking full communion,
that they may become sharers in the promise of Christ through the gospel.

FOR THE CHRISTIAN ASSEMBLY
For this eucharistic assembly, that we may faithfully offer Christ the gold of a living faith,
the incense of our worship and the myrrh of compassion for others.

FOR THE DEAD
For those who followed the star of faith and walked by the light of Christ (especially N.),
that, joyfully entering heaven, they may behold God face to face.

Introduction to the Lord's Prayer

Because in Christ we have received the Spirit of adoption,
as sons and daughters of God we dare to pray:

Invitation to Holy Communion

Behold the true Light of the world, the Beloved of God, anointed by the Spirit.
Blessed are those who are called to the banquet of the Lamb.

Dismissal

Enlightened by Christ and anointed by the Spirit, go now in peace to love and serve the Lord.

BAPTISM OF THE LORD

FIRST SUNDAY AFTER THE EPIPHANY

Father of great and everlasting glory,
by the power of your Holy Spirit
you have consecrated your Word made flesh
and have established this Christ, our Savior,
    as the Light of the world,
your covenant of peace for all the peoples.

As we celebrate today
the mystery of Jesus' baptism in the river Jordan,
renew in us our own baptism:
Pattern our lives on this Christ,
the One you have specially chosen,
the One on whom your favor rests,
the Beloved with whom you are well pleased.

We ask this through our Lord Jesus Christ, your Son
who lives and reigns with you
in the unity of the Holy Spirit,
God for ever and ever.

Lord our God, O Holy One of Israel,
to the waters you call all those who thirst,
to the feast of your covenant you invite
    all the nations.

As once at the Jordan your Spirit tore open
    the heavens,
and your voice proclaimed Jesus your well-beloved
    Son,
so now call us by name, your beloved sons and
    daughters;
lead us by your Spirit through the water and the
    blood,
that our love for you may strengthen us to obey your
    commandments,
and our love for one another be the victory that
    forever conquers the world.

We ask this through our Lord Jesus Christ,
Emmanuel, God with us,
your Son who lives and reigns with you
in the unity of the Holy Spirit,
God for ever and ever.

Roman Lectionary
Isaiah 55:1–11 *or* 42:1–4, 6–7
Psalm 29:1–4, 8–10
1 John 5:1–9 *or* Acts 10:34–38
Mark 1:7–11

Revised Common Lectionary
Genesis 1:1–5
Psalm 29
Acts 19:1–7
Mark 1:4–11

General Intercessions

In prayer let us call on God who draws near to us in Christ,
the Beloved One on whom God's Spirit rests.

That all who are baptized into the everlasting covenant
may conquer the world by faith and transform it by love.

FOR THE WORLD
That nations who do not yet know God's steadfast love
may be moved by the witness of believers to seek and find the Lord.

FOR THOSE OPPRESSED, AFFLICTED OR IN NEED
That those estranged from God and from the community may forsake their wicked ways
and return to the God of mercy who abundantly pardons.

That those unsatisfied by material gain, who thirst for fulfillment,
may come to drink freely the wine of God's kingdom and the milk of God's wisdom.

FOR THE NEEDS OF THE LOCAL COMMUNITY
That those in our religious education and sacramental preparation programs
may incline their ears to the word of life
and find delight at God's feast and love among God's children.

That the catechumens (of our community) may come with Jesus through water and blood
and receive the Spirit's anointing as God's beloved sons and daughters.

FOR THE CHRISTIAN ASSEMBLY
That God's word, descending on us like winter's snow and rain,
may accomplish its purpose among us and yield a harvest of obedient faith and generous love.

FOR THE DEAD
That all the departed who believed in Jesus as the Christ (especially N.)
may share fully in the victory by which Christ conquers death.

Introduction to the Lord's Prayer

Because in Christ we have received the Spirit of adoption,
as sons and daughters of God we dare to pray:

Invitation to Holy Communion

Behold the true Light of the world, the Beloved of God, anointed by the Spirit.
Blessed are those who are called to the banquet of the Lamb.

Dismissal

Enlightened by Christ and anointed by the Spirit,
go now in peace to love and serve the Lord.

ASH WEDNESDAY

At this, the acceptable time,
O God so rich in mercy,
we gather in solemn assembly
to receive the announcement of the lenten spring,
and the ashes of mortality and repentance.

Lead the elect, exulting, to the waters of salvation;
guide the penitent, rejoicing, to the healing river;
carry us all to the streams of renewal.

We ask this through Christ,
our reconciliation and our peace,
who lives and reigns with you
in the unity of the Holy Spirit,
God for ever and ever.

Merciful God of infinite compassion,
whose creating power called us forth from the dust
    of the earth
and whose redeeming love fashioned us anew
    in your divine image,
in this, the acceptable time,
lead us inward to be at peace with you,
impel us outward to be reconciled with our neighbor,
that we may embrace the sacred discipline of Lent
with broken, humbled hearts
and so come to the blessed joy of the paschal feast
cleansed and renewed.

We ask this through our Lord Jesus Christ, your Son,
who lives and reigns with you
in the unity of the Holy Spirit,
God for ever and ever.

Roman Lectionary	Revised Common Lectionary
Joel 2:12–18	Joel 2:1–2, 12–17 *or* Isaiah 58:1–12
Psalm 51: 5–6, 12–14, 17	Psalm 51:1–17
2 Corinthians 5:20 — 6:2	2 Corinthians 5:20b — 6:10
Matthew 6:1–6, 16–18	Matthew 6:1–6, 16–21

General Intercessions

Assembled to begin the lenten journey toward the joyful paschal feast,
let us return with all our hearts to the God who is gracious and merciful,
slow to anger and abounding in steadfast love.

FOR THE CHURCH
That the Lord may sanctify the church's fast,
purifying the church inwardly, strengthening its witness among the nations.

FOR THE WORLD
That enemies may be reconciled to God and to one another, recognizing the lenten spring as God's
acceptable time, the day of salvation.

FOR THOSE OPPRESSED, AFFLICTED OR IN NEED
That the plight of the distressed and afflicted may rend our hardened hearts,
renewing our resolve to be ambassadors of Christ's compassion.

That those estranged from God or the assembly may return,
finding God's blessing awaiting them, and the welcome of God's people.

FOR THE NEEDS OF THE LOCAL COMMUNITY
That the elect may accept the grace of God in this season,
experiencing Lent with us as a fruitful time of enlightenment and renewal.

FOR THE CHRISTIAN ASSEMBLY
That we may pray, fast and give alms as the gospel teaches,
making this Lent the springtime of salvation.

FOR THE DEAD
That our Father who sees in secret may reward the faithful departed (especially N.),
granting them a full share in Christ's paschal victory.

Introduction to the Lord's Prayer

BAPTISMAL
Baptized into Christ's death that we might share in the resurrection,
let us pray for the fulfillment of this mystery as Jesus taught us:

PENITENTIAL
While we were still sinners, Christ died for us,
that, with confidence in God's love for us, we might dare to pray:

Invitation to Holy Communion

Behold the Righteous One, who was put to death in the flesh but made alive in the spirit.
Blessed are those who are called to the banquet of the Lamb.

◆

Behold the Christ, in whom we have become a new creation, in whom God is reconciling the world.
Blessed are those who are called to the banquet of the Lamb.

Dismissal

Saved by faith and created in Christ for good works,
go in peace to love and serve the Lord.

◆

Reconciled to God through Christ and made a new creation,
go in peace to love and serve the Lord.

◆

FIRST SUNDAY OF LENT

Your bow, O God, is set in the clouds,
a sign of the covenant between you and the earth.
The cross of Christ is traced on our foreheads,
a sign of the mystery that seals our lives.

Bring us through these forty days
in the power of Christ's victory,
as at the font of living water
the elect find new birth,
the penitent find pardon,
and all of us rejoice.

We ask this through Christ,
the pioneer and perfecter of our faith,
the Lord who lives and reigns with you
in the unity of the Holy Spirit,
God for ever and ever.

Gracious God, ever true to your covenant,
whose loving hand sheltered Noah and the
    chosen few
while the waters of the great flood
cleansed and renewed a fallen world,
may we, sanctified through the saving waters
    of baptism
and clothed in the shining garments of immortality,
be touched again by our call to conversion
and give our lives anew to the challenge of your reign.

We ask this through our Lord Jesus Christ, your Son,
who lives and reigns with you
in the unity of the Holy Spirit,
God for ever and ever.

Roman Lectionary
Genesis 9:8–15
Psalm 25:4–9
1 Peter 3:18–22
Mark 1:12–15

Revised Common Lectionary
Genesis 9:8–17
Psalm 25:1–10
1 Peter 3:18–22
Mark 1:9–15

General Intercessions

Saved by baptism and called to share Christ's victory over temptation,
let us offer our intercession to God.

FOR THE CHURCH
That these forty days in the wilderness of Lent
may increase the church's strength for proclaiming the good news.

FOR THE WORLD
That God's covenant of peace with all flesh
may inspire nations to prepare a heritage of peace for future generations.

FOR THOSE OPPRESSED, AFFLICTED OR IN NEED
That we who share this planet with every living creature
may be good stewards of this fragile ark and reverence it as God's creation.

That the elect, who draw near to the saving waters of baptism,

may persevere in the covenant that God is establishing with them.

FOR THE CHRISTIAN ASSEMBLY

That all the baptized, led by the Spirit and one with Jesus,

may experience the lenten wilderness as a place of testing and triumph.

FOR THE DEAD

That, having departed this life with a good conscience, our beloved dead (especially N.)

may go with Christ into heaven to the right hand of God.

Introduction to the Lord's Prayer

BAPTISMAL

Baptized into Christ's death that we might share in the resurrection,

let us pray for the fulfillment of this mystery as Jesus taught us:

PENITENTIAL

While we were still sinners, Christ died for us,

that, with confidence in God's love for us, we might dare to pray:

Invitation to Holy Communion

Behold the Righteous One, who was put to death in the flesh but made alive in the spirit.

Blessed are those who are called to the banquet of the Lamb.

◆

Behold the Christ, in whom we have become a new creation, in whom God is reconciling the world.

Blessed are those who are called to the banquet of the Lamb.

Dismissal

Saved by faith and created in Christ for good works,

go in peace to love and serve the Lord.

◆

Reconciled to God through Christ and made a new creation,

go in peace to love and serve the Lord.

◆

SECOND SUNDAY OF LENT

God of Abraham and of Jesus,
on the holy mountain you have provided
a lamb for the atonement of our sin,
an intercessor to plead for your people,
a beloved Son, transfigured,
as the pledge of our salvation.

It is good for us to be here!
Let us listen to your Son
and bear witness in the world
to that love from which nothing can separate us.

We ask this through Christ,
the pioneer and perfecter of our faith,
the Lord who lives and reigns with you
in the unity of the Holy Spirit,
God for ever and ever.

God of all goodness,
you did not spare your only-begotten son
but gave him up for the sake of us sinners.
Strengthen within us the gift of obedient faith,
that, in all things, we may follow faithfully in
    Christ's footsteps,
and, with him, be transfigured in the light of
    your glory.

We ask this through our Lord Jesus Christ, your Son,
who lives and reigns with you
in the unity of the Holy Spirit,
God for ever and ever.

Roman Lectionary	**Revised Common Lectionary**
Genesis 22:1–2, 9a, 10–13, 15–18	Genesis 17:1–7, 15–16
Psalm 116:10, 15–19	Psalm 22:23–31
Romans 8:31b–34	Romans 4:13–25
Mark 9:2–10	Mark 8:31–38 *or* 9:2–9

General Intercessions

To the God who did not withhold his own Son but gave him up for us,
let us offer our intercessions.

FOR THE CHURCH
That the people of God enduring persecution or tested by suffering
may behold in the Lord's transfiguration the pledge of paschal victory.

FOR THE WORLD
That the angel of God may stay the hand of powers and interests
that threaten to sacrifice peace in a holocaust of hate.

That the lenten penance of Christians may bear fruit
in practical charity for the victims of hardship and distress.

FOR THE NEEDS OF THE LOCAL COMMUNITY
That the elect may listen to the voice of God's Beloved Son
and by obedient faith share in the blessings promised to Abraham.

FOR THE CHRISTIAN ASSEMBLY
That we may always leave this holy mountain of word and worship
with new vigor for bearing witness to the victory of the risen Christ.

FOR THE DEAD
That Christ Jesus who died and was raised to the right hand of God
may lead to transfigured glory all of our beloved departed (especially N.).

Introduction to the Lord's Prayer

BAPTISMAL
Baptized into Christ's death that we might share in the resurrection,
let us pray for the fulfillment of this mystery as Jesus taught us:

PENITENTIAL
While we were still sinners, Christ died for us,
that, with confidence in God's love for us, we might dare to pray:

Invitation to Holy Communion

Behold the Righteous One, who was put to death in the flesh but made alive in the spirit.
Blessed are those who are called to the banquet of the Lamb.

◆

Behold the Christ, in whom we have become a new creation, in whom God is reconciling the world.
Blessed are those who are called to the banquet of the Lamb.

Dismissal

Saved by faith and created in Christ for good works,
go in peace to love and serve the Lord.

◆

Reconciled to God through Christ and made a new creation,
go in peace to love and serve the Lord.

◆

THIRD SUNDAY OF LENT

YEAR B

O God, whose foolishness is wise
and whose weakness is strong,
by the working of your grace
in the disciplines of Lent
cleanse the temple of your church
and purify the sanctuary of our hearts.

Let zeal for your house consume us
and obedience to your commandments absorb us,
that we may come to the Easter festival
prepared to renew our baptismal covenant.

We ask this through Christ,
your power and your wisdom,
the Lord who lives and reigns with you
in the unity of the Holy Spirit,
God for ever and ever.

Holy is your name, O Lord our God.
Incline our hearts to keep your commandments,
and school us in the sublime wisdom of the cross,
so that, free from sin,
which imprisons us in our own self-centeredness,
we may open ourselves to the gift of your Spirit
and become living temples of your love.

We ask this through our Lord Jesus Christ, your Son,
who lives and reigns with you
in the unity of the Holy Spirit,
God for ever and ever.

Roman Lectionary	Revised Common Lectionary
Exodus 20:1–17 *or* 20:1–3, 7–8, 12–17	Exodus 20:1–17
Psalm 19: 8–11	Psalm 19
1 Corinthians 1:22–25	1 Corinthians 1:18–25
John 2:13–25	John 2:13–22

General Intercessions

Let us come in prayer before the Lord our God, whose steadfast love embraces all generations.

FOR THE CHURCH
That the temple of God's church may ever be cleansed from within
and fashioned more perfectly as the living image of the risen Christ.

FOR THE WORLD
That those who control worldly power and shape human wisdom
may attend to the law of God and respond to the needs of the lowly.

FOR THOSE OPPRESSED, AFFLICTED OR IN NEED
That the innocent victims of greed and violence may find, in Christ crucified,
new strength in their suffering and, in Christ's disciples, wise allies in their struggle.

That those among us whose work is in the marketplace
may witness to the truth of the commandments, the wisdom of the gospel.

FOR THE CHRISTIAN ASSEMBLY
That our lenten observance may increase our zeal for God's house
and deepen our dedication to the word Jesus has spoken.

FOR THE DEAD
That those who in life were fashioned as living stones
into the temple of Christ's body (especially N.)
may be raised up from death to eternal joy with Christ.

Introduction to the Lord's Prayer

BAPTISMAL
Baptized into Christ's death that we might share in the resurrection,
let us pray for the fulfillment of this mystery as Jesus taught us:

PENITENTIAL
While we were still sinners, Christ died for us,
that, with confidence in God's love for us, we might dare to pray:

Invitation to Holy Communion

Behold the Righteous One, who was put to death in the flesh but made alive in the spirit.
Blessed are those who are called to the banquet of the Lamb.

◆

Behold the Christ, in whom we have become a new creation, in whom God is reconciling the world.
Blessed are those who are called to the banquet of the Lamb.

Dismissal

Saved by faith and created in Christ for good works,
go in peace to love and serve the Lord.

◆

Reconciled to God through Christ and made a new creation,
go in peace to love and serve the Lord.

◆

THIRD SUNDAY OF LENT

YEAR A
SUNDAY OF THE FIRST SCRUTINY

O God, you loved us while we were yet sinners;
in Christ you come in search of us.
We thirst for your grace.

As once at Moses' hand in the desert,
as once at Jacob's well with the Samaritan woman,
so now make your gift of faith in all of us,
elect and baptized,
a spring of living water, leaping up to eternal life.

We ask this through Christ,
whose gifts are water, light and life,
the Lord who lives and reigns with you
in the unity of the Holy Spirit,
God for ever and ever.

O God, the living fountain of new life,
to the human race, parched with thirst,
you offer the living water of grace
that springs up from the rock, our Savior Jesus
    Christ.
Grant your people the gift of the Spirit,
that we may learn to profess our faith with courage
    and conviction
and announce with joy the wonders of your saving
    love.

We ask this through our Lord Jesus Christ, your Son,
who lives and reigns with you
in the unity of the Holy Spirit,
God for ever and ever.

Roman Lectionary	Revised Common Lectionary
Exodus 17:3 – 7	Exodus 17:1 – 7
Psalm 95: 1 – 2, 6 – 9	Psalm 95
Romans 5:1 – 2, 5 – 8	Romans 5: 1 – 11
John 4:5 – 42 *or* 4:5 – 15, 19b – 26, 39a, 40 – 42	John 4:5 – 42

General Intercessions

Let us pray to God, whose love has been poured into our hearts,
through the Holy Spirit that has been given to us.

FOR THE CHURCH
That in the wilderness of this world
the church may be the rock of God, providing the waters of life to all who thirst.

FOR THE WORLD
That those who control worldly power and shape human wisdom
may attend to the law of God and respond to the needs of the lowly.

That the innocent victims of greed and violence may find in Christ crucified
new strength in their suffering and, in Christ's disciples, wise allies in their struggle.

FOR THE NEEDS OF THE LOCAL COMMUNITY
That the Messiah may bestow on our elect
the living water that will become a spring leaping up to eternal life.

FOR THE CHRISTIAN ASSEMBLY
That our lenten observance may prepare us to renew our baptismal vows,
and with the elect, to profess Jesus as the Christ, the Savior of the world.

FOR THE DEAD
That (N.) and all those who in life were fashioned as living stones into the temple of Christ's body
may be raised up from death to eternal joy with Christ.

Introduction to the Lord's Prayer

Baptized into Christ's death that we might share in the resurrection,
let us pray for the fulfillment of this mystery as Jesus taught us:

Invitation to Holy Communion

Behold the Righteous One, who was put to death in the flesh but made alive in the spirit.
Blessed are those who are called to the banquet of the Lamb.

◆

Behold the Christ, in whom we have become a new creation, in whom God is reconciling the world.
Blessed are those who are called to the banquet of the Lamb.

Dismissal

Saved by faith and created in Christ for good works,
go in peace to love and serve the Lord.

◆

Reconciled to God through Christ and made a new creation,
go in peace to love and serve the Lord.

◆

FOURTH SUNDAY OF LENT

YEAR B

God of mercy,
who sent your Son into the world
not to condemn it but to save it,
open our eyes to behold Jesus lifted up on the cross
and to see in those outstretched arms
your abundant compassion.

Let the world's weary and wounded come to know
that by your gracious gift we are saved and delivered,
so immeasurable is the love with which you love
   the world.

We ask this through Christ,
with whom you have raised us up in baptism,
the Lord who lives and reigns with you
in the unity of the Holy Spirit,
God for ever and ever.

O God, ever faithful and kind to all,
with tireless love you call the wayward home,
inviting them back to the path of true conversion;
and in your Son, lifted up on the cross,
you have provided us with healing
from the sting of the Evil One.
Grant us the abundant riches of your grace,
that, with our spirits renewed,
we may be able to respond
to your boundless and eternal love.

We ask this through our Lord Jesus Christ, your Son,
who lives and reigns with you
in the unity of the Holy Spirit,
God for ever and ever.

Roman Lectionary
2 Chronicles 36:14–17, 19–23
Psalm 137:1–6
Ephesians 2:4–10
John 3:14–21

Revised Common Lectionary
Numbers 21:4–9
Psalm 107:1–3, 17–22
Ephesians 2:1–10
John 3:14–21

General Intercessions

Let us offer our intercessions to the God who is rich in mercy.

FOR THE CHURCH
That the church, the house of God,
may be built up by the challenge of prophetic voices and the fidelity of God's people.

FOR THE WORLD
That God, who so loved the world that he gave his only Son,
may banish deeds of darkness from our society by the light of truth.

FOR THOSE OPPRESSED, AFFLICTED OR IN NEED

That lands made desolate by war and refugees driven from their homes by conflict
may come to a sabbath of healing and a season of peace.

FOR THE NEEDS OF THE LOCAL COMMUNITY

That God's healing power may work through medical personnel
who dedicate themselves to the physical and emotional wholeness of others.

FOR THE CHRISTIAN ASSEMBLY

That we who are saved by faith may live as children of light,
rich in good works as our way of life in Christ Jesus.

FOR THE DEAD

That the dead (especially N.) may be raised up and seated with Christ
in the glory of the heavenly places.

Introduction to the Lord's Prayer

BAPTISMAL

Baptized into Christ's death that we might share in the resurrection,
let us pray for the fulfillment of this mystery as Jesus taught us:

PENITENTIAL

While we were still sinners, Christ died for us,
that with confidence in God's love for us, we might dare to pray:

Invitation to Holy Communion

Behold the Righteous One, who was put to death in the flesh but made alive in the spirit.
Blessed are those who are called to the banquet of the Lamb.

◆

Behold the Christ, in whom we have become a new creation, in whom God is reconciling the world.
Blessed are those who are called to the banquet of the Lamb.

Dismissal

Saved by faith and created in Christ for good works,
go in peace to love and serve the Lord.

◆

Reconciled to God through Christ and made a new creation,
go in peace to love and serve the Lord.

FOURTH SUNDAY OF LENT

YEAR A
SUNDAY OF THE SECOND SCRUTINY

O God whose face we long to see,
in Christ you come in search of us,
judging not by outward appearance
but gazing into our hearts
at the light you have kindled.

As once you gave Samuel insight
to see young David as your shepherd-king,
as once you led the man born blind
to look on Christ and behold the face of your
   Anointed,
so now clear our vision and focus our sight
that all of us, the elect and the baptized,
may acknowledge Christ as the Light of the world.

We ask this through Christ,
whose gifts are water, light and life,
the Lord who lives and reigns with you
in the unity of the Holy Spirit,
God for ever and ever.

O God, the author and source of all light,
you gaze into the depths of our inmost hearts.
Never permit the powers of darkness
to hold your people captive,
but open our eyes by the grace of your Spirit,
that we may be able to look on your Son
and see the One you sent to illumine the world,
so that, seeing, we may believe and worship Jesus as
   the Lord
who lives and reigns with you
in the unity of the Holy Spirit,
God for ever and ever.

Roman Lectionary
1 Samuel 16:1, 6 – 7, 10 – 13
Psalm 23:1– 6
Ephesians 5:8 –14
John 9:1– 41 *or* 9:1, 6 – 9, 13 –17, 34 – 38

Revised Common Lectionary
1 Samuel 16:1–13
Psalm 23
Ephesians 5:8 –14
John 9:1– 41

General Intercessions

In the presence of God, whose light shines on us in Christ,
let us intercede now for the needs of all.

FOR THE CHURCH
That the church may scatter earth's darkness with the light of Christ
by preaching the just word and practicing what we preach.

FOR THE WORLD

That God, who so loved the world that he gave his only Son,
may banish deeds of darkness from our society by the light of truth.

FOR THOSE OPPRESSED, AFFLICTED OR IN NEED

That lands made desolate by war, and refugees driven from their homes by conflict,
may come to a sabbath of healing and a season of peace.

FOR THE NEEDS OF THE LOCAL COMMUNITY

That the elect may be enlightened and reveal God's mighty works to the world through their witness.

FOR THE CHRISTIAN ASSEMBLY

That our lenten observance may wake us from sleep and fill us with light
to bring forth all that is good and right and true.

FOR THE DEAD

That the dead (especially N.) may be raised up with Christ and seated in the glory of heaven.

Introduction to the Lord's Prayer

Baptized into Christ's death that we might share in the resurrection,
let us pray for the fulfillment of this mystery as Jesus taught us:

Invitation to Holy Communion

Behold the Righteous One, who was put to death in the flesh but made alive in the spirit.
Blessed are those who are called to the banquet of the Lamb.

◆

Behold the Christ, in whom we have become a new creation, in whom God is reconciling the world.
Blessed are those who are called to the banquet of the Lamb.

Dismissal

Saved by faith and created in Christ for good works,
go in peace to love and serve the Lord.

◆

Reconciled to God through Christ,
go in peace to love and serve the Lord.

FIFTH SUNDAY OF LENT

YEAR B

Deep within our hearts, O God,
you have written your law,
and high upon the cross
you have lifted up our salvation,
the Savior made perfect in suffering.

From the death of that single grain
sown in the weary earth,
bring forth in this lenten springtime
a rich harvest of life.
As the hour of his passion draws near,
glorify your name,
and in our baptismal renewal,
let it be glorified again.

We ask this through Christ,
the pioneer and perfecter of our faith,
the Lord who lives and reigns with you
in the unity of the Holy Spirit,
God for ever and ever.

Hear, O God, the eternal echo
of the prayers and supplications
your Son offered when,
to establish the new and everlasting covenant,
he became obedient even unto death on the cross.
Through all the trials of this life,
bring us to a deeper, more intimate share
in Christ's redeeming passion,
that we may produce the abundant fruit of that seed
that falls to the earth and dies,
and so be gathered as your harvest for the kingdom of
   heaven.

We ask this through our Lord Jesus Christ, your Son,
who lives and reigns with you
in the unity of the Holy Spirit,
God for ever and ever.

Roman Lectionary	**Revised Common Lectionary**
Jeremiah 31:31–34	Jeremiah 31:31–34
Psalm 51:3–4, 12–15	Psalm 51:1–12 *or* Psalm 119:9–16
Hebrews 5:7–9	Hebrews 5:5–10
John 12:20–33	John 12:20–33

General Intercessions

Let us offer up prayers and supplications to God through Jesus
who has become the source of our eternal salvation.

FOR THE CHURCH
   That all the people of God, from the least to the greatest,
   may know the Lord through the law of love written in their hearts.

That the judgment of this world
may herald justice for the oppressed.

FOR THOSE OPPRESSED, AFFLICTED OR IN NEED

That the afflicted, who offer their prayers with loud cries and tears,
may find strength in their union with Jesus, who was made perfect through suffering.

FOR THE NEEDS OF THE LOCAL COMMUNITY

That teachers, lawyers, social workers and others with special skills
may use their gifts for the poor and disenfranchised.

FOR THE CHRISTIAN ASSEMBLY

That those hoping to see Jesus
may find the Son of Man glorified among us in our celebration and service.

FOR THE DEAD

That those who have been sown with Christ in death (especially N.)
may bear an abundant harvest with Christ in eternal life.

Introduction to the Lord's Prayer

Let us pray in the name and in the words of Jesus,
who learned obedience through what he suffered:

Invitation to Holy Communion

Behold the Servant of God, obedient unto death on a cross, highly exalted as Lord of glory.
Blessed are those who are called to the banquet of the Lamb.

Dismissal

Confessing that Jesus is Lord, to the glory of God,
go forth in the peace of Christ.

FIFTH SUNDAY OF LENT

YEAR A
SUNDAY OF THE THIRD SCRUTINY

As once in the vision, O God,
your prophet summoned the spirit
so that dry bones stood up alive,
and as once your Son stood fearless at death's door
calling Lazarus to come forth alive,
raise us up with Christ from the death of sin,
that all of us, the elect and the baptized,
may be unbound and set free.

We ask this through Christ,
whose gifts are water, light and life,
the Lord who lives and reigns with you
in the unity of the Holy Spirit,
God for ever and ever.

O God of eternal life,
whose glory is the human person fully alive,
in the tears that Jesus shed for Lazarus his friend
we see the living incarnation
of your tenderness and compassion.
Graciously behold the distress of your church,
which mourns and prays as a mother
for her children whose sins have brought them death.
By the power of your Spirit,
call them back to life,
unbind them and let them go free.

We ask this through our Lord Jesus Christ, your Son,
who lives and reigns with you
in the unity of the Holy Spirit,
God for ever and ever.

Roman Lectionary
Ezekiel 37:12–14
Psalm 130:1–8
Romans 8:8–11
John 11:1–45 *or* 11:3–7, 17, 20–27, 33b–45

Revised Common Lectionary
Ezekiel 37:1–14
Psalm 130
Romans 8:6–11
John 11:1–45

General Intercessions

Let us pray to God, who raised Jesus from the dead
as the resurrection and the life of all who believe.

FOR THE CHURCH
That wherever the power of death holds people bound
the church may summon forth life in the name of Christ.

FOR THE WORLD
That the judgment of this world
may herald justice for the oppressed.

FOR THOSE OPPRESSED, AFFLICTED OR IN NEED

That those who mourn the loss of loved ones
may experience the comfort of Christ in the presence of the community.

FOR THE NEEDS OF THE LOCAL COMMUNITY

That in the sacraments of baptism, confirmation and the eucharist our elect will experience Christ,
who calls them to life, unbinds them and lets them go free.

FOR THE CHRISTIAN ASSEMBLY

That through penance and reconciliation
this assembly may be raised from the grave and filled with God's spirit.

FOR THE DEAD

That the faithful who have gone to their rest (especially N.)
may hear the voice of Jesus calling them forth to life and resurrection.

Introduction to the Lord's Prayer

Let us pray in the name and in the words of Jesus,
who learned obedience through what he suffered:

Invitation to Holy Communion

Behold the Servant of God, obedient unto death on a cross, highly exalted as Lord of glory.
Blessed are those who are called to the banquet of the Lamb.

Dismissal

Confessing that Jesus is Lord, to the glory of God,
go forth in the peace of Christ.

PASSION (PALM) SUNDAY

Your Servant, Lord our God, speaks the word
that all the weary long to hear.
Your Son humbles himself to carry the cross
that your people long to embrace.

As we enter this Holy Week,
let the same mind be in us that was in Christ Jesus.
Empty us of ourselves,
and draw us close to the cross of Christ,
that, looking on One forsaken,
we may acknowledge this man to be truly
    the Son of God
and confess him as Christ and Lord.

We ask this through your Son, the Christ,
our Passover and Peace,
who lives and reigns with you
in the unity of the Holy Spirit,
God for ever and ever.

O God, for whom all things are possible,
you have highly exalted your suffering Servant,
who did not hide from insult
but humbled himself even to death on a cross.

As we begin the journey of Holy Week,
take our sin away by Christ's glorious passion
and confirm our worship and witness,
so that when we proclaim the name of Jesus,
every knee shall bend and every tongue proclaim
that Jesus Christ is Lord.

We ask this through your Son, the Christ,
our Passover and Peace,
who lives and reigns with you
in the unity of the Holy Spirit,
God for ever and ever.

Roman Lectionary

PROCESSION WITH PALMS

> Mark 11:1–10
> *or*
> John 12:12–16

MASS

> Isaiah 50:4–7
> Psalm 22:8–9, 17–20, 23–24
> Philippians 2:6–11
> Mark 14:1—15:47 *or* 15:1–39

Revised Common Lectionary

LITURGY OF THE PALMS

> Mark 11:1–11
> *or*
> John 12:12–16
> Psalm 118:1–2, 19–29

LITURGY OF THE PASSION

> Isaiah 50:4–9a
> Psalm 31:9–16
> Philippians 2:5–11
> Mark 14:1—15:47 *or* 15:1–39, (40–47)

General Intercessions

In the name of Jesus, the name that is above every name,
let us offer our intercessions to God:

FOR THE CHURCH

That the church, teaching in the name of Christ,
may sustain the weary with a word of courage, righteousness and hope.

FOR THE WORLD

That civil authorities may listen to the voices that cry out for food,
for dignity and for peace.

FOR THOSE OPPRESSED, AFFLICTED OR IN NEED

That those who face insult and degradation because of race, religious belief or political opinion
may be supported by disciples of the Lord, who took the form of a slave.

FOR THE NEEDS OF THE LOCAL COMMUNITY

That we may accompany the elect to the waters of baptism,
supporting them by our prayer and fasting, and confessing with them that Jesus Christ is Lord.

FOR THE CHRISTIAN ASSEMBLY

That, as we celebrate Holy Week and the Triduum,
we may empty ourselves like Christ Jesus, serving in unselfish love.

FOR THE DEAD

That those who by their sufferings shared in the passion of Christ (especially N.)
may share fully in the victory of Christ's exaltation.

Introduction to the Lord's Prayer

Let us pray in the name and in the words of Jesus,
who learned obedience through what he suffered:

Invitation to Holy Communion

Behold the Servant of God, obedient unto death on a cross, highly exalted as Lord of glory.
Blessed are those who are called to the banquet of the Lamb.

Dismissal

Confessing that Jesus is Lord, to the glory of God,
go forth in the peace of Christ.

HOLY THURSDAY

With joy, O God of salvation,
the assembly of your holy people
begins the Three Day Pasch,
in which Christ manifests the gospel
in his own flesh and blood.

Stir our hearts by the example of this Savior,
who welcomed to his table
even those who would betray, deny and desert him,
the Lord who knew their weaknesses
yet bent down to wash their feet.

We ask this through your Son, the Christ,
our Passover and Peace,
who lives and reigns with you
in the unity of the Holy Spirit,
God for ever and ever.

To learn the mystery of sacrificial love, O God,
we come to the supper hosted by your Son,
to the table where the sinless One
delights to eat and drink with sinners.

Touch our hearts with wonder
to see the Lord enwrapped in glory
tie a towel about his waist,
the Master whom raging seas obey
pour water into a servant's basin,
the One whom angels wait on,
kneel down to wash the disciples' feet.
As we enter this Three Day Pasch,
cleanse us within
that we may keep the festival
not with the old yeast of malice and evil
but with the unleavened bread of sincerity and truth.

We ask this through your Son, the Christ, our
    Passover and Peace,
who lives and reigns with you
in the unity of the Holy Spirit,
God for ever and ever.

Roman Lectionary
Exodus 12:1–8, 11–14
Psalm 116:12–13, 15–18
1 Corinthians 11:23–26
John 13:1–15

Revised Common Lectionary
Exodus 12:1–4, (5–10), 11–14
Psalm 116:1–2, 12–19
1 Corinthians 11:23–26
John 13:1–17, 31b–35

General Intercessions

As we enter into the Passover of the Lord,
let us intercede before God on behalf of all in the name of Jesus, our Teacher and Lord.

FOR THE CHURCH
For the church, the household of faith redeemed by the blood of the Lamb:
May it celebrate this Triduum as a festival of deliverance and new life.

FOR THE WORLD

For the world God loved so much that he gave his only Son:
May God execute judgment on the false gods of power and greed.

FOR THOSE OPPRESSED, AFFLICTED OR IN NEED

For those enslaved by powers without or by forces within:
May they find freedom in Christ's love and support from Christ's disciples.

FOR THE ELECT

For those about to be baptized into Christ's paschal mystery:
May their washing in those saving waters give them a full share with Christ.

FOR THE SICK AND HOMEBOUND

For the sick and homebound of this community (especially N.) and for
    those who take the eucharist to them:
May their communion with us in Christ be a source of healing and strength.

FOR THE MINISTRIES OF CHARITY

For those whose works of charity in this community fulfill Christ's example of humility and service:
May Christ's gift of the eucharist sustain their gift of love to others.

FOR PRIESTS

For those ordained to preside at the altar of Christ's sacrifice and supper:
May they fulfill by lives of service the love they celebrate in these mysteries.

FOR THE CHRISTIAN ASSEMBLY

For all of us gathered in remembrance of Christ to proclaim his death until he comes:
May our joy and hope be in Christ who loves his own in this world and who will love us to the end.

FOR THE DEAD

For those who have departed this world to go to the Father (especially N.):
May they come to share fully in Christ's paschal victory.

Introduction to the Lord's Prayer

With trust in God whose providence nourishes and sustains us,
we pray now as Jesus taught us:

Invitation to Holy Communion

Behold the living bread come down from heaven: Those who eat of it will never die.
Behold the cup of eternal life: Those who drink of it will live for ever.

GOOD FRIDAY

Prostrate on the ground,
your Son prayed, O God,
that this hour might pass,
this cup be taken away.
But then he rose to do your will,
to stretch out his arms on the cross,
to be lifted up from the earth
and to be glorified by you.

Prostrate before you, O God,
we ponder the mystery of your saving will.
In this hour of Christ's exaltation, we beg you:
Open our hearts
to hear the story of our salvation,
to stretch out our hands in prayer,
to venerate the cross by which the whole world is
    lifted up
to salvation, life and resurrection.

We ask this through your Son, the Christ,
our Passover and Peace,
who lives and reigns with you
in the unity of the Holy Spirit,
God for ever and ever.

At this hour, O God Most High,
while silence reigns
and the sun hides its face,
a world prostrate beneath its sins
lifts its eyes to the cross,
rejoicing that the tree of knowledge,
which brought the human race to its knees,
has become the tree of life,
lifting us up to redemption.

Let the glorious cross forever stand
as the sign of our worth in your eyes!
As we behold Innocence itself
crucified in place of the guilty
and Life put to death for sinners,
may we take heart,
remembering the prayer of the dying thief
whose faith was rewarded.

We ask this through your Son, the Christ,
our Passover and Peace,
who lives and reigns with you
in the unity of the Holy Spirit,
God for ever and ever.

Roman Lectionary	**Revised Common Lectionary**
Isaiah 52:13 — 53:12	Isaiah 52:13 — 53:12
Psalm 31:2, 6, 12 –13, 15 – 17, 25	Psalm 22
Hebrews 4:14 –16, 5:7 – 9	Hebrews 10:16 – 25 *or* 4:14 –16; 5:7 – 9
John 18:1 —19:42	John 18:1 — 19:42

The Universal Prayer

FOR THE HOLY CHURCH

For God's holy church now, dearly beloved, let us pray:
The Lord our God grant peace to it and make it one,
and keep it safe throughout the whole wide world,

that we, serenely living in the quiet peace God gives,
may glorify and praise almighty God.

Pause for silent prayer

Almighty and everlasting God,
who have revealed your glory to all the world in Christ,
your merciful design pursue!
Wide as the world your church is scattered,
yet still, with unchanging faith,
may it persevere in the confession of your name.
This we pray through Christ our Lord.

FOR THE POPE

For our Holy Father, Pope N., now let us pray:
The Lord our God who chose him to be bishop
for holy church's sake preserve him safe and sound,
the appointed shepherd of God's holy people.

Pause for silent prayer

Almighty and everlasting God,
on whose decree all things depend,
in your mercy hear us,
and in your love protect the pope whom you have chosen.
Under his pastoral care may we, the Christian people,
your own flock, evermore increase in living faith.
This we pray through Christ our Lord.

FOR ALL IN HOLY ORDERS AND ALL THE FAITHFUL

For N., the bishop of this church, now let us pray:
For all the bishops, presbyters and deacons,
for all who serve in varied ministries,
and for all God's holy people, let us pray.

Pause for silent prayer

Almighty and everlasting God,
by whose spirit the whole body of your church
is sanctified and guided on its journey,
listen to our prayers for all within it,
in all our rich diversity of callings.
Your grace for all, we pray,
each member, every ministry.
May all our service ever faithful be and ever fruitful!
This we pray through Christ our Lord.

◆

For our beloved catechumens and the elect now let us pray:
The Lord our God open their ears and hearts to the word,
open wide the floodgates of his mercy.
Set free from sin by the cleansing of new birth,
may these new brothers and sisters be numbered with us
in Jesus Christ our Lord.

Pause for silent prayer

Almighty and everlasting God,
by whose grace the church's womb
is fruitful with new offspring every year:
ever more faith grant to our catechumens
and ever more discernment.
In the pure font of baptism born anew,
may they be always counted among your children of adoption.
This we pray through Christ our Lord.

FOR CHRISTIAN UNITY

For all brothers and sisters who share our faith in Christ now let us pray:
The Lord our God bring us to deeper unity and keep us all together,
one holy church that seeks to live one truth.

Pause for silent prayer

Almighty and everlasting God,
whose plan it is to gather what has been scattered
and to preserve as one what you have gathered:
To the flock of Christ your Son give heed!
One baptism, even now, share we in common,
which sanctifies and forms us as your own.
Soon may our common heritage embrace as well
one faith professed in all its fullness,
one bond of charity by all held dear.
This we ask through Christ our Lord.

FOR THE JEWISH PEOPLE

For the Jewish people, too, now let us pray:
The chosen people, before all others,
by God's decree, they are!
Ever deeper be the love they bear
for the name they do not speak, so great their reverence,
and ever more faithful may they be to the covenant they cherish.

Pause for silent prayer

Almighty and everlasting God,
whose promises were sworn to Abraham and Sarah
and to their posterity through countless generations:
To your church's prayers now graciously attend!
Firstborn were they among the children of your covenant;
full, too, may their share be in the mystery of redemption
when, at last, all your promises are graciously fulfilled.
This we ask through Christ our Lord.

FOR THOSE WHO DO NOT BELIEVE IN CHRIST
For those who do not yet believe in Christ now let us pray:
The light of the Holy Spirit shine on them,
and into salvation's pathway guide their feet.

Pause for silent prayer

Almighty and everlasting God,
for those who, with sincerity of heart,
walk always in your presence,
let every path explored and each step taken
lead always, surely, finally, to the Truth.
Use us for this, your work of grace!
Ever more genuine may our love for one another be
and thus ever more convincing our witness
to your steadfast love at work in all the world.
This we ask through Christ our Lord.

FOR THOSE WHO DO NOT BELIEVE IN GOD
For those, too, who do not yet believe in God, now let us pray:
Sincere and single-hearted be their quest for truth,
and may all the paths by which they seek the truth
lead them to God.

Pause for silent prayer

Almighty and everlasting God,
our hearts are restless, for you have made them so.
And you have made them to be restless until they rest in you.
Many the obstacles that hide your face from mortal eyes!
But let each worthy witness, each good work done by believers,
be for the skeptical and the unbelieving
a glimpse of your face lighting their way
toward the joy of believing in you.
This we ask through Christ our Lord.

For all who hold public office now let us pray:
The Lord our God direct their minds and hearts
toward peace that is real, freedom that is true
and all the good gifts God wills for this world's happiness.

Pause for silent prayer

Almighty and everlasting God,
whose hands embrace the whole wide world,
shielding each heart and its unspoken longings,
upholding every human right that we hold dear:
Enfold in your gracious governance
all this world's powers and authorities.
Let peace reign over all the earth,
and with that peace, a shared prosperity,
freedom from fear,
and freedom, too, of worship.
This we ask through Christ our Lord.

FOR THOSE IN ANY NEED

Finally, dear friends, to God the Father almighty let us pray:
For a world where falsehood is no more, we pray;
for an end to ravages of famine, epidemic and disease;
for a stop to crime and violence, we pray;
for the liberation of every shackled mind and body,
safe shelter for the traveler, for pilgrims a happy homecoming,
healing for the sick and a peaceful passage home to God
for those now at death's door.

Pause for silent prayer

Almighty and everlasting God,
for all the world's afflicted, you are counselor and comfort;
for those bent down beneath life's burdens,
you are hope and courage born new each morning.
Disfigured now with pain is the face of our weary earth,
the heavens echoing no more angelic songs of peace
but cries of pain instead, your children's anguish.
Give ear and heed, O Lord our God, and answer for his sake,
the One whose death cry from the cross tore heaven open.
Let the victory of your Christ transform our crosses, one and all!
Your mighty arm lift up the fallen!
Your loving kindness heal and soothe and make earth whole again!
This we pray through Christ our Lord.

Introduction to the Lord's Prayer

With our eyes fixed on Jesus, whose blood was shed for our redemption,
let us seek pardon and peace from God as we pray:

Invitation to Holy Communion

Behold the Servant of God, obedient unto death on a cross, highly exalted as Lord of glory.
Blessed are those who are called to the banquet of the Lamb.

HOLY SATURDAY

God of mighty power,
living forever and source of all life,
your only Son descended to the realm of the dead,
so that from that abode of exile and shadow
you might raise him up to new life
and to glory at your side.

Let all those who in faith
descend into the waters of baptism
find the font of the church to be
both the tomb in which they die with Christ to sin
and the womb from which they rise reborn,
    a new creation.

We ask this through your Son, the Christ,
our Passover and Peace,
who lives and reigns with you
in the unity of the Holy Spirit,
God for ever and ever.

O God for whom the whole creation lives
and in whose hands are the depths of earth
and the heights of the mountains,
the crucified body of your beloved Son
was laid in a new tomb, hewn from the rock,
    in a garden,
and rested on this holy Sabbath day.

As your church awaits with Christ
the dawning of the third day
and the beginning of your new creation,
grant that all who are buried with Christ
in the waters of baptism
may rise with Christ to new life
and find their perfect rest in that glorious kingdom
that Christ has established by his paschal mystery.

We ask this through your Son, the Christ,
our Passover and Peace,
who lives and reigns with you
in the unity of the Holy Spirit,
God for ever and ever.

Roman Tradition

CANADIAN LECTIONARY
> Zechariah 12:10 –11, 13:6 – 7 *or*
> Ephesians 2:13 – 18

LITURGY OF THE HOURS
> Psalms 4, 16, 24
> Hebrews 4:1–13

MONASTIC OFFICE
> Year I: Lamentations 5:1– 22
> Year II: Jeremiah 20:7–18

CHRISTIAN INITIATION
> *Recitation of the Creed*
> Matthew 16:13 –17 *or* John 6:35, 63 – 71
> *Ephphetha Rite*
> Mark 7:31-37

Baptismal Name
> Genesis 17:1– 7 *or* Isaiah 62:1– 5 *or* Revelation
> 3:11–13 *or* Matthew 16:13 –18 *or* John 1:40 – 42

Revised Common Lectionary

> Job 14:1–14 *or* Lamentations 3:1– 9, 19 – 24 *or*
> Hebrews 10:12 – 23
> Psalm 31:1– 4, 15 –16
> 1 Peter 4:1– 8
> Matthew 27:57– 66
> *or*
> John 19:38 – 42

General Intercessions

Let us intercede for all the world through our Intercessor and Redeemer, Jesus Christ,
who for our sake suffered death, was buried and rose again.

FOR THE CHURCH
For the church, keeping watch at the Lord's tomb:
In fasting, vigil and prayer may your people ready their own hearts
and help prepare the whole church to celebrate
that holy night in which light and fire, water and word, bread and wine give birth to new life.

FOR THE WORLD
For the world, bearing the scars of humanity's continuing sin:
May Christ, the new Adam, who harrows hell and liberates the just,
extend that victory throughout the world, banishing evil and setting free the oppressed.

FOR THE ELECT
For the elect of the church, awaiting the waters of baptism:
May the power of the risen Christ lead them
and the persevering prayer of this community accompany them
to the sacred mysteries by which they are reborn and the church is renewed.

FOR THOSE OPPRESSED, AFFLICTED OR IN NEED
For all whom death and decay in any form hold bound:
May they, like Christ's sorrowing mother, join their sufferings to his passion
and find them transformed by Christ's sacrificial and redemptive love.

FOR THE CHRISTIAN ASSEMBLY
For all of us meditating on Christ's suffering and death in hope of resurrection:
May we await the harvest of the seed fallen to the earth and sown in death
and bear with Christ a rich harvest in the joy and peace of the paschal spring.

FOR THE DEAD
For those who, like Christ, go to the tomb as to the entranceway of glory (especially N.):
May the Lord, who encompasses the universe but chose to be confined in the tomb,
set free our faithful departed and the whole human race for resurrection to undying life.

Introduction to the Lord's Prayer

With our eyes fixed on Jesus, whose blood was shed for our redemption,
let us seek pardon and peace from God as we pray:

EASTER VIGIL

O God, Creator and Fountain of life,
from the moment your Spirit hovered over the
    primal waters
to this night when baptism's life-giving waters flow,
you have been at work,
forming a people as your own,
breathing life into the work of your hands
and making the whole creation new.

Tonight with water and oil,
with bread and wine,
and with our very lives,
continue to fashion salvation:
Flood the world with the undying life
of your Son, our Lord Jesus Christ,
the faithful witness, the firstborn from the dead,
who lives and reigns with you
in the unity of the Holy Spirit,
God for ever and ever.

This night, O God, is different from all others,
for in all other nights
the daylight fades as dark descends.
But on this night undying Light is kindled,
the night turns into day,
and the glory of the Lord dawns in the resurrection,
and creation is born anew.

Number our elect among that new creation,
and seal them as your own forever.
Lead us all
to the table where Love has set a feast
and into the world Love has redeemed.

We ask this through your Son, the Christ,
our Passover and Peace,
who lives and reigns with you
in the unity of the Holy Spirit,
God for ever and ever.

Roman Lectionary

Genesis 1:1— 2:2 or 1:1, 26 – 31a
Psalm 104:1– 2, 5 – 6, 10, 12 –14, 24, 35
or Psalm 33:4 – 7, 12 –13, 20 – 22
Genesis 22:1–18 or 22:1– 2, 9a, 10 –13, 15 –18
Psalm 16:5, 8 – 11
Exodus 14:15 —15:1
Exodus 15:1– 6, 17–18
Isaiah 54:5 –14
Psalm 30:2, 4 – 6, 11 – 13
Isaiah 55:1–11
Isaiah 12:2 – 6
Baruch 3:9 –15, 32 — 4:4
Psalm 19: 8 – 11
Ezekiel 36:16 –17a, 18 – 28
Psalm 42:3, 5; 43:3, 4
Romans 6:3 –11
Psalm 118:1– 2, 16, 17, 22 – 23
Mark 16:1– 8

Revised Common Lectionary

Genesis 1:1 — 2:4a
Psalm 136:1– 9, 23 – 26
Genesis 7:1– 5, 11–18; 8:6 –18; 9:8 –13
Psalm 46
Genesis 22:1–18
Psalm 16
Exodus 14:10 – 31; 15:20 – 21
Exodus 15:1b –13, 17–18
Isaiah 55: 1– 11
Isaiah 12:2 – 6
Baruch 3:9 –15, 32 — 4:4 or Proverbs 8:1– 8, 19 – 21; 9:4b – 6
Psalm 19
Ezekiel 36:24 – 28
Psalm 42 and 43
Ezekiel 37:1–14
Psalm 143
Zephaniah 3:14 – 20
Psalm 98
Romans 6:3 –11
Psalm 114
Mark 16:1– 8

General Intercessions

In the radiant splendor of this most holy night,
let us cry out to the Lord whose mighty deeds we have seen
in the deliverance of God's people through the resurrection of Jesus Christ.

FOR THE CHURCH
For the people of God, brought through saving waters to a land of promise:
May our lives be a song of joy to the Lord who has triumphed gloriously.

FOR THE WORLD
For all the human race, created in the image and likeness of God:
May God place within all peoples a new heart and a new spirit.

FOR THOSE OPPRESSED, AFFLICTED OR IN NEED
For innocent victims of terror and oppression:
May violence be banished and righteousness with prosperity be restored.

FOR THE NEOPHYTES
For those newly baptized into the death and resurrection of Christ:
May they walk always with Christ in newness of life.

FOR THE NEEDS OF THE LOCAL COMMUNITY
For those who feel abandoned in their affliction:
May God's great compassion gather them into the care of this community.

FOR THE DEAD
For the faithful departed whose life-long vigil for the Lord has ended (especially N.):
May those who have died with Christ also live with him.

Introduction to the Lord's Prayer

Because in Christ we have received the Spirit of adoption,
as sons and daughters of God we dare to pray:

Invitation to Holy Communion

Alleluia! Christ our paschal lamb has been sacrificed. Therefore, let us keep the festival.
Blessed are those who are called to the banquet of the Lamb.

Dismissal

Go forth and bear witness to Christ,
who is gloriously risen from the dead, Alleluia, Alleluia!

EASTER SUNDAY

Day

This is the day, Lord God, that you have made!
Raising Christ from the dead,
and raising us with Christ,
you have fashioned for yourself a new people,
washed in the flood of baptism,
sealed with gift of the Spirit,
invited to the banquet of the Lamb!

In the beauty of this Easter morning,
set our minds on the new life
to which you have called us;
place on our lips the words of witness
for which you have anointed us;
and ready our hearts to celebrate the festival,
with the unleavened bread of sincerity and truth.

We ask this through your Son, the Christ,
our Passover and Peace,
who lives and reigns with you
in the unity of the Holy Spirit,
God for ever and ever.

Evening

In the setting sun of this day that you have made,
Lord God,
your church on its journey,
we disciples on our pilgrimage,
implore your Son,
stay with us, Lord!

As we hear the word that brings salvation,
make our hearts burn within us.
In the breaking of the bread,
open our eyes to recognize the One whose feast it is.
Through the presence of every friend and stranger,
reveal to us the face of the one who had first to suffer
but who has entered now into glory:
your Son, the Lord Jesus Christ,
    our Passover and our Peace.
who lives and reigns with you
in the unity of the Holy Spirit,
God for ever and ever.

Roman Lectionary
Acts 10:34a, 37–43
Colossians 3:1–4
or
1 Corinthians 5:6b–8
DAY
        John 20:1–9
        or
        Mark 16:1–7
EVENING
        Luke 24:13–35

Revised Common Lectionary
DAY
        Acts 10:34–43 *or* Isaiah 25:6–9
        Psalm 118:1–2, 14–24
        1 Corinthians 15:1–11 *or* Acts 10:34–43
        John 20:1–18 *or* Mark 16:1–8
EVENING
        Isaiah 25:6–9
        Psalm 114
        1 Corinthians 5:6b–8
        Luke 24:13–49

General Intercessions

On this, the day the Lord has made, let us rejoice and be glad
as we pray to the God who raised Jesus from the dead.

For the people of God, brought through saving waters to a land of promise:
May we joyfully proclaim, with our lips and our lives,
the good news of Christ's victory over sin and death.

FOR THE WORLD

For all the peoples of earth during this festival of Christ's resurrection:
May the gloom of malice and evil yield to a springtime of sincerity and truth.

FOR THOSE OPPRESSED, AFFLICTED OR IN NEED

For those bound by sin or oppressed by evil:
May forgiveness of sins and spiritual freedom be theirs with Easter joy.

FOR THE NEOPHYTES

For those newly baptized into the death and resurrection of Christ:
May they walk always with Christ in newness of life.

FOR THE NEEDS OF THE LOCAL COMMUNITY

For those who are sick or homebound (especially N.):
May the risen Christ visit them with healing power and new hope.

FOR THE ASSEMBLY

For this assembly, gathered to eat and drink with the risen Lord:
May we set our hearts on things that are above even as we bear witness here to the risen Christ.

FOR THE DEAD

For those who have died and whose lives are hidden with Christ in God (especially N.):
May they live forever with Christ in the glory of the resurrection.

Introduction to the Lord's Prayer

Because in Christ we have received the Spirit of adoption,
as sons and daughters of God, we dare to pray:

Invitation to Holy Communion

Alleluia! Christ our paschal lamb has been sacrificed. Therefore, let us keep the festival.
Blessed are those who are called to the banquet of the Lamb.

Dismissal

Go forth and bear witness to Christ,
who is gloriously risen from the dead, Alleluia, Alleluia!

SECOND SUNDAY OF EASTER

One in mind and heart, O God of glory,
your people gather to proclaim your steadfast love,
to proclaim the risen Christ
in whom we are baptized.

Let the peace that Christ bestowed
on the first disciples
reign now over this assembly.
Let the Spirit breathed on them
fill our hearts anew.

We ask this through the Lord Jesus,
our Passover and our Peace,
who lives and reigns with you
in the unity of the Holy Spirit,
God for ever and ever.

Each Sunday, O God,
as we celebrate the weekly Pasch,
we relive the wonders of your marvelous work
    of salvation
and experience anew the power of Christ's
    Easter victory.

By the grace of your Spirit,
help us to recognize the Lord
who comes into our assembly and stands among us,
so that as a community of believers,
one in mind and heart,
we may with great power give our testimony
to the resurrection of the Lord Jesus Christ,
who lives and reigns with you
in the unity of the Holy Spirit,
God for ever and ever.

Roman Lectionary	Revised Common Lectionary
Acts 4:32–35	Acts 4:32–35
Psalm 118:2–4, 13–15, 22–24	Psalm 133
1 John 5:1–6	1 John 1:1—2:2
John 20:19–31	John 20:19–31

General Intercessions

Gathered as believers who are one in heart and soul,
let us pray through Jesus, the Son of God, gloriously risen from the dead.

FOR THE CHURCH
That the church may give testimony to the resurrection of the Lord Jesus
by its love of God and its generous care for those in need.

FOR THE WORLD
That world leaders may find the means to conquer mistrust
with mutual respect and understanding.

FOR THOSE OPPRESSED, AFFLICTED OR IN NEED

That the homeless and dispossessed may find among today's Christians
the same generosity that marked the community at its beginnings.

FOR THE NEOPHYTES

That the neophytes, born of God in the sacraments of initiation,
may always find joy in their new life in Jesus the Messiah.

FOR THE NEEDS OF THE LOCAL COMMUNITY

That those among us blessed with resources of our own
may generously share with others as any have need.

FOR THE CHRISTIAN ASSEMBLY

That we who have not seen the risen Lord and yet have come to believe
may be blessed in sharing the peace and forgiveness we have received.

FOR THE DEAD

That those who in life believed Jesus to be the Christ, the Son of God (especially N.)
may now rejoice and be glad in God's steadfast love that endures forever.

Introduction to the Lord's Prayer

Because in Christ we have received the Spirit of adoption,
as sons and daughters of God, we dare to pray:

Invitation to Holy Communion

Alleluia! Christ our paschal lamb has been sacrificed. Therefore, let us keep the festival.
Blessed are those who are called to the banquet of the Lamb.

Dismissal

Go forth and bear witness to Christ,
who is gloriously risen from the dead, Alleluia, Alleluia!

THIRD SUNDAY OF EASTER

God of Jesus Christ, the holy and righteous One,
by that suffering graciously borne
and that victory gloriously bestowed,
you extend to us all
what you promised through the prophets.

Renew in this assembly the wonders of your power:
Open our minds to understand the scriptures,
make Jesus known to us in the breaking of the bread.

We ask this through the Lord Jesus,
our Passover and our Peace,
who lives and reigns with you
in the unity of the Holy Spirit,
God for ever and ever.

God of Abraham and Sarah,
God of Isaac and Rebekah,
God of Jacob and Rachel and of all our ancestors
    in faith,
you have glorified your servant Jesus
and made him the atoning sacrifice for our sins,
the source of peace and reconciliation for the
    whole world.

Open our hearts to true conversion,
and as we have known the Lord in the breaking of
    the bread
so make us witnesses of a new humanity,
renewed, reconciled and at peace in your love.
Send us as heralds of the repentance and forgiveness
you offer to all in the name of your Son Jesus Christ,
who lives and reigns with you
in the unity of the Holy Spirit,
God for ever and ever.

Roman Lectionary
Acts 3:13–15, 17–19
Psalm 4:2, 4, 7–9
1 John 2:1–5a
Luke 24:35–48

Revised Common Lectionary
Acts 3:12–19
Psalm 4
1 John 3:1–7
Luke 24:36b–48

General Intercessions

To the God of our ancestors who has glorified his servant Jesus,
let us pray not only for our own needs but also those of the whole world.

FOR THE CHURCH
For all members of the church in every ministry:
May we proclaim to all nations repentance and forgiveness of sins in the name of Jesus.

For worldly rulers who in ignorance reject God's Holy One and make the disciples suffer:
May they repent and turn to God.

FOR THOSE OPPRESSED, AFFLICTED OR IN NEED

For those depressed by the burden of their sins:
May they come to know that in Jesus Christ the righteous they have an advocate.

FOR THE NEOPHYTES

For the neophytes (here and) throughout the church:
May the love of God reach perfection in them.

FOR THE NEEDS OF THE LOCAL COMMUNITY

For believers whose hearts are filled with doubts:
May they find comfort in God's word and joy at the eucharistic feast.

FOR THE CHRISTIAN ASSEMBLY

For us to whom the Lord has been made known in the breaking of the bread:
May we be effective witnesses to the peace Christ has bestowed on us.

FOR THE DEAD

For those who, in union with Jesus, endured suffering, and for all the departed (especially N.):
May they be now with the Author of life, whom God raised from the dead.

Introduction to the Lord's Prayer

Because in Christ we have received the Spirit of adoption,
as sons and daughters of God, we dare to pray:

Invitation to Holy Communion

Alleluia! Christ our paschal lamb has been sacrificed. Therefore, let us keep the festival.
Blessed are those who are called to the banquet of the Lamb.

Dismissal

Go forth and bear witness to Christ,
who is gloriously risen from the dead, Alleluia, Alleluia!

FOURTH SUNDAY OF EASTER

What love you have bestowed on us, O God,
that we should be called your children,
born again in Christ by water and the Spirit.

What love you have lavished
that we should be gathered
into the fold of a Shepherd
whose life is given freely for us.
Keep us safe, make us one,
and gather all your scattered children
into the one fold of this one Shepherd.

We ask this through the Lord Jesus,
our Passover and our Peace,
who lives and reigns with you
in the unity of the Holy Spirit,
God for ever and ever.

Creator God,
you make the resplendent glory of the Risen One
shine with new radiance on the world,
whenever our human weakness is healed and restored.

Gather all your scattered children
into one flock following Christ, our Good Shepherd,
so that all may taste the joy you bestow
on those who are the children of God.

We ask this through our Lord Jesus Christ, your Son,
who lives and reigns with you
in the unity of the Holy Spirit,
God for ever and ever.

Roman Lectionary	**Revised Common Lectionary**
Acts 4:8 –12	Acts 4:5 –12
Psalm 23: 1– 6	Psalm 23
1 John 3:1– 2	1 John 3:16 – 24
John 10:11–18	John 10:11–18

General Intercessions

Let us intercede for the needs of all God's children
in the name of Jesus the Good Shepherd.

FOR THE CHURCH
That all those outside the fold, for whom Jesus laid down his life,
may be gathered into the one flock of the one Shepherd.

FOR THE WORLD
That those who control the destinies of nations
may act as responsible stewards of the power and people entrusted to their care.

FOR THOSE OPPRESSED, AFFLICTED OR IN NEED

That society's defenseless ones
may be known and defended by Christians as God's own, worthy of dignity and respect.

FOR THE NEOPHYTES

That those newly baptized into the one flock of the Lord may rejoice in the salvation that is theirs.

FOR THE NEEDS OF THE LOCAL COMMUNITY

That those who are sick (especially N.)
may find health in the name of Jesus and care at the hands of his disciples.

FOR THE CHRISTIAN ASSEMBLY

That we who know and are known by the Good Shepherd
may gladly welcome into this flock all who will listen to the Lord's voice.

FOR THE DEAD

That all the departed who were God's children by baptism (especially N.)
may become like God in eternal life.

Introduction to the Lord's Prayer

Because in Christ we have received the Spirit of adoption,
as sons and daughters of God we dare to pray:

Invitation to Holy Communion

Alleluia! Christ our paschal lamb has been sacrificed. Therefore, let us keep the festival.
Blessed are those who are called to the banquet of the Lamb.

Dismissal

Go forth and bear witness to Christ,
who is gloriously risen from the dead, Alleluia, Alleluia!

◆

FIFTH SUNDAY OF EASTER

Your love for us, O God, surpasses our poor hearts,
and your command is only this:
that we should become true disciples
by believing in Jesus and loving one another.

Grafted now as living branches of Christ
    the true Vine,
may we be pruned and cultivated by your care
and so glorify you by bearing much fruit
in the midst of the church.

We ask this through the Lord Jesus,
our Passover and our Peace,
who lives and reigns with you
in the unity of the Holy Spirit,
God for ever and ever.

As a Vinegrower, O God, you have grafted us
    onto Christ,
that we may abide as living branches joined
    to the true Vine.

Bestow on us the comforting presence of your
    Holy Spirit,
so that, loving one another with a love that is sincere,
we may become the firstfruits of a humanity
    made new
and bear a rich harvest whose fruits are holiness
    and peace.

We ask this through our Lord Jesus Christ, your Son,
who lives and reigns with you
in the unity of the Holy Spirit,
God for ever and ever.

Roman Lectionary	**Revised Common Lectionary**
Acts 9:26–31	Acts 8:26–40
Psalm 22:26–28, 30–32	Psalm 22:25–31
1 John 3:18–24	1 John 4:7–21
John 15:1–8	John 15: 1–8

General Intercessions

Grafted as living branches onto Christ the true Vine,
let us ask God to provide for the needs of all.

FOR THE CHURCH
For the church in all its communities throughout the world:
May it have peace and be built up in this paschal season.

FOR THE WORLD
For the families of nations in all their rich diversity:
May peoples seek peace not in word or speech only but in truth and action.

FOR THOSE OPPRESSED, AFFLICTED OR IN NEED

For those whose hearts condemn them to despair:
May the God who is greater than our hearts reassure them with pardon and peace.

FOR THE NEOPHYTES

For the newly initiated Christians:
May they glorify the Father by bearing fruit.

FOR THE NEEDS OF THE LOCAL COMMUNITY

For those whom the Vinegrower is pruning by sickness, suffering or trials (especially N.):
May they persevere through this cleansing and see their yield increase.

FOR THE CHRISTIAN ASSEMBLY

For this community's increase in faith and numbers:
May we live in the fear of the Lord and in the comfort of the Holy Spirit.

FOR THE DEAD

For those departed who obeyed the commandments and did what pleased God (especially N.):
May they receive from God the eternal life for which they asked.

Introduction to the Lord's Prayer

Because in Christ we have received the Spirit of adoption,
as sons and daughters of God we dare to pray:

Invitation to Holy Communion

Alleluia! Christ our paschal lamb has been sacrificed. Therefore, let us keep the festival.
Blessed are those who are called to the banquet of the Lamb.

Dismissal

Go forth and bear witness to Christ,
who is gloriously risen from the dead, Alleluia, Alleluia!

SIXTH SUNDAY OF EASTER

Your love, O God, is revealed among us
in the gift of your Son Jesus,
who laid down his life
and bestows on us the joy
of abiding in your love.

Baptized into Christ,
we pray that through the witness we bear
you will bring forth fruit that will last,
and teach us, God of love, how to love one another.

We ask this through the Lord Jesus,
our Passover and our Peace,
who lives and reigns with you
in the unity of the Holy Spirit,
God for ever and ever.

In this is love, O God: not that we have loved you
but that you have first loved us
and sent your only Son into the world
so that we might live through Christ.

Teach us, by your Spirit,
to live as the Lord's true friends,
and to love one another as Jesus has loved us,
even to the point of sacrificial love,
knowing that there can be no greater love
than to lay down one's life for one's friends.

We ask this through our Lord Jesus Christ, your Son,
who lives and reigns with you
in the unity of the Holy Spirit,
God for ever and ever.

Roman Lectionary

*In the Catholic archdioceses and dioceses of Canada and
of the states of Alaska, California, Hawaii, Idaho, Montana,
Nevada, Oregon, Utah and Washington, the Ascension
of the Lord is transferred to the following Sunday. The second
reading and gospel of the Seventh Sunday of Easter may be
read on the Sixth Sunday of Easter.*

Acts 10:25 – 26, 34 – 35, 44 – 48
Psalm 98:1, 2 – 4
1 John 4:7–10
John 15:9 –17

Revised Common Lectionary

Acts 10:44 – 48
Psalm 98
1 John 5:1– 6
John 1:9 –17

General Intercessions

Let us offer our intercession to the God who has first loved us and sent the Son
to be the atoning sacrifice for our sins.

FOR THE CHURCH
That the church may gladly welcome to the waters of baptism
those of every nation who fear God and do what is acceptable to God.

That nations with plentiful resources may open their borders freely,
imitating the generous hospitality of God, who shows no partiality.

FOR THOSE OPPRESSED, AFFLICTED OR IN NEED
That all who by lives of service make themselves friends to those in need
may be signs to us of Christ, who laid down his life for his friends.

FOR THE NEOPHYTES
That the neophytes, called by Christ in baptism and chosen to be friends,
may go forth from this paschal season to bear fruit that will last.

FOR THE NEEDS OF THE LOCAL COMMUNITY
That those preparing to receive the outpouring of the Holy Spirit
may extol God and bear witness to God's gift by their love for others.

FOR THE CHRISTIAN ASSEMBLY
That we who have been born of God and know the God who is love
may fulfill Christ's command to love one another as Christ has loved us.

FOR THE DEAD
That all the dead who kept the commandments and abided in Christ's love (especially N.)
may know forever the joy of Christ.

Introduction to the Lord's Prayer

Because in Christ we have received the Spirit of adoption,
as sons and daughters of God we dare to pray:

Invitation to Holy Communion

Alleluia! Christ our paschal lamb has been sacrificed. Therefore, let us keep the festival.
Blessed are those who are called to the banquet of the Lamb.

Dismissal

Go forth and bear witness to Christ,
who is gloriously risen from the dead, Alleluia, Alleluia!

ASCENSION OF THE LORD

God of all creation,
whose mighty power raised Jesus from the dead,
be present to this community of disciples
gathered in one Lord, one faith, one baptism.

Maintain us in the unity of the Spirit,
and keep us bound in peace.
Build up the church
to the full stature of Christ,
and so let the whole world know
the good news of healing power.

We ask this in the name of the Lord Jesus,
who intercedes before you on our behalf,
living and reigning with you
in the unity of the Holy Spirit,
God for ever and ever.

You have glorified your Christ, O God,
exalting to your right hand the Son
who emptied himself for us in obedience unto death
   on the cross,
and thus have exalted
all of us who have been baptized
into Christ's death and resurrection.

Clothe us now with power from on high
that we may proclaim the good news to the world,
confirming our message by the sign of our love
   for one another,
and maintaining the unity of the Spirit in the bond
   of peace.

We ask this through our Lord Jesus Christ, your Son,
who lives and reigns with you
in the unity of the Holy Spirit,
God for ever and ever.

Roman Lectionary
*In the Catholic archdioceses and dioceses of Canada and
of the states of Alaska, California, Hawaii, Idaho, Montana,
Nevada, Oregon, Utah and Washington, the Ascension of
the Lord is transferred to the following Sunday.*
Acts 1:1–11
Psalm 47: 2 – 3,6 – 9
Ephesians 4:1–13 *or* 4:1– 7, 11–13 *or* 1:17–23
Mark 16:15 – 20

Revised Common Lectionary
Acts 1:1–11
Psalm 47 *or* Psalm 93
Ephesians 1:15 – 23
Luke 24:44 – 53

General Intercessions

Let us offer our petitions through the Lord Jesus,
who was taken up to heaven and intercedes for us at the right hand of God.

FOR THE CHURCH
For all who share one Lord, one faith, one baptism:
Adorned with a rich variety of gifts, may the church bear witness to the ends of the earth.

FOR THE WORLD

For all races and nations:

May the children of the one God and Father of all make every effort to maintain the unity of the Spirit in the bond of peace.

FOR THOSE OPPRESSED, AFFLICTED OR IN NEED

For prisoners of conscience and others held captive:

By the gift of grace, may they persevere in humility and patience.

FOR THE NEOPHYTES

For the neophytes, baptized with the Holy Spirit and called to witness:

Together may we and they come to the maturity of the full stature of Christ.

FOR THE NEEDS OF THE LOCAL COMMUNITY

For the apostles, prophets, evangelists, pastors and teachers
in this community and throughout the church:

May their work of ministry build up the body of Christ in unity of faith.

FOR THE CHRISTIAN ASSEMBLY

For this community's mission to go forth and proclaim the good news:

May we sense the Lord working with us and confirming the message.

FOR THE DEAD

For those taken from our sight by death (especially N.):

May they be with Christ in glory at the right hand of God.

Introduction to the Lord's Prayer

Because in Christ we have received the Spirit of adoption,
as sons and daughters of God we dare to pray:

Invitation to Holy Communion

Alleluia! Christ our paschal lamb has been sacrificed. Therefore, let us keep the festival.
Blessed are those who are called to the banquet of the Lamb.

Dismissal

Go forth and bear witness to Christ,
proclaiming the good news to all, Alleluia, Alleluia!

SEVENTH SUNDAY OF EASTER

O God, by whose name we are protected,
sanctify in truth
the disciples gathered by Jesus
to be your people in the world.

Pour out your Spirit every day,
that, remaining in this world but not belonging to it,
we may bear witness to your own abiding love,
made known to us in our Savior Jesus Christ,
who lives and reigns with you
in the unity of the Holy Spirit,
God for ever and ever.

O God, the inexhaustible fountain of life,
you accepted the offering of your Son
who gave his life as a sacrifice
for the salvation of the world.

Sanctify us in the truth
and consecrate us in that unity
that is your Spirit's gift,
that we may abide always in your love
and be witnesses of the resurrection.

We ask this through our Lord Jesus Christ, your Son,
who lives and reigns with you
in the unity of the Holy Spirit,
God for ever and ever.

Roman Lectionary	**Revised Common Lectionary**
Acts 1:15–17, 20a, 20c–26	Acts 1:15–17, 21–26
Psalm 103:1–2, 11–12, 19–20	Psalm 1
1 John 4:11–16	1 John 5:9–13
John 17:11b–19	John 17:6–19

General Intercessions

Knowing and believing the love God has for us,
let us offer intercession in the name of Jesus.

FOR THE CHURCH
That the people of God, sent into the world to bear witness,
may be protected from the Evil One and sanctified in the truth.

FOR THE WORLD
That worldly powers who hate the word of truth and its servants
may be touched and transformed by the Lord who knows every heart.

FOR THOSE OPPRESSED, AFFLICTED OR IN NEED
That Christians may seek out those who feel unloved or neglected
and bear witness to the God who is love.

That the neophytes, numbered now among the believers,
may ever abide in God by confessing that Jesus is the Son of God.

FOR THE NEEDS OF THE LOCAL COMMUNITY
That those chosen for ministry and apostleship in the church
may be effective witnesses to Christ's resurrection and God's abiding love.

FOR THE CHRISTIAN ASSEMBLY
That this community may bear witness that because God has loved us
so we also must love one another.

FOR THE DEAD
That the departed who believed in Christ (especially N.)
may have Christ's joy made complete in them.

Introduction to the Lord's Prayer

Because in Christ we have received the Spirit of adoption,
as sons and daughters of God we dare to pray:

Invitation to Holy Communion

Alleluia! Christ our paschal lamb has been sacrificed. Therefore, let us keep the festival.
Blessed are those who are called to the banquet of the Lamb.

Dismissal

Go forth and bear witness to Christ,
proclaiming the good news to all, Alleluia, Alleluia!

PENTECOST SUNDAY
VIGIL

O God of the covenant,
you revealed yourself on the holy mountain in fire
and on Pentecost in the flame of the Holy Spirit.
Let your mighty fire burn away our pride,
consume our hatreds, annihilate the armaments
    of death
and kindle instead, within the whole human family,
the welcomed fire of your love.

We ask this through our Lord Jesus Christ, your Son,
who lives and reigns with you
in the unity of the Holy Spirit,
God for ever and ever.

Today, O God, you bring to fulfillment
the paschal mystery of Jesus your Son.
Pour forth your Holy Spirit on the church
that it may be a living Pentecost throughout history
and to the very ends of the earth.
Gather all nations and peoples as one
to believe, to hope and to love.

We ask this through our Lord Jesus Christ, your Son,
who lives and reigns with you
in the unity of the Holy Spirit,
God for ever and ever.

Roman Lectionary
For an extended vigil, all the readings listed may be read.
In Canada the readings of Pentecost Day are used at
the first Mass of Pentecost Sunday (Saturday evening).

Genesis 11:1– 9
Psalm 33:10 –15
or
Exodus 19:3 – 8a, 16 – 20b
Daniel 3:52 – 56
or
Ezekiel 37:1–14
Psalm 107: 2 – 9
or
Joel 3:1– 5
Psalm 104: 1– 2a, 24, 25c, 27– 28, 29bc – 30
Psalm 104:1– 2, 24, 35, 27– 28, 30
Romans 8:22 – 27
John 7:37– 39

General Intercessions

On the last day of the great Fifty Days of Easter, let us pray to God who searches the heart,
knowing that the Spirit intercedes for the saints according to God's will.

FOR THE CHURCH

That the church may gather into unity at the table of the Lord
people of every race and language and way of life.

FOR THE WORLD

That God's Spirit may bestow on old and young alike
dreams of peace and visions of justice.

FOR THOSE OPPRESSED, AFFLICTED OR IN NEED

That God's Spirit may breathe the new life of hope
into those deprived of freedom, devastated by hunger or denied their human dignity.

FOR THE NEOPHYTES

That those baptized into the life of the covenant
may persevere as members of God's priestly people and holy nation.

FOR THE NEEDS OF THE LOCAL COMMUNITY

That those who labor on behalf of the physically or mentally handicapped
may see their efforts as part of the birth pangs of the Spirit's new creation.

FOR THE CHRISTIAN ASSEMBLY

That we who have gathered for the culmination of the paschal feast
may drink deeply the living water of God's Spirit and bear faithful witness.

FOR THE DEAD

That those who went to their graves believing in Christ's resurrection (especially N.)
may be raised by the power of God's Spirit to the joy of eternal life.

Introduction to the Lord's Prayer

Because in Christ we have received the Spirit of adoption,
as sons and daughters of God we dare to pray:

Invitation to Holy Communion

Alleluia! Christ our paschal lamb has been sacrificed. Therefore, let us keep the festival.
Blessed are those who are called to the banquet of the Lamb.

Dismissal

Go forth in the power of the Spirit,
proclaiming the good news of Christ to all, Alleluia, Alleluia!

PENTECOST SUNDAY

In every generation, O God of Easter glory,
you send forth your holy Creator Spirit,
to breathe on the world your love has fashioned
and to make it come alive!

Fulfill the promise of these Fifty Days
with the abundant harvest of your Spirit's gifts.
Bring forth in the lives of all of us
born of water and the Spirit,
the love, joy and peace your Spirit's fire bestows.

We ask this through our Lord Jesus Christ,
who sends us the Spirit of truth from you,
and who lives and reigns with you
in the unity of the Holy Spirit,
God for ever and ever.

You open wide your hand, O God,
and satisfy with your good gifts
the needs of all who live.
Pour forth your Holy Spirit on your church,
gathered in prayer with the mother of Jesus,
and cause springs of living water to well up within it,
so that all may quench their thirst for justice
    and truth.

We ask this through our Lord Jesus Christ, your Son,
who lives and reigns with you
in the unity of the Holy Spirit,
God for ever and ever.

Roman Lectionary

Acts 2:1–11
Psalm 104:1, 24, 29 – 31, 34
1 Corinthians 12:3b – 7, 12 –13
or
Galatians 5:16 – 25
John 20:19 – 23 *or* 15:26 – 27; 16:12 –15

Revised Common Lectionary

If the passage from Ezekiel is chosen for the first reading, the passage from Acts is used as the second reading.
Acts 2:1– 21
or
Ezekiel 37:1–14
Psalm 104:24 – 34, 35b
Romans 8:22 – 27
or
Acts 2:1– 21
John 15:26 – 27; 16:4b –15

General Intercessions

Filled with the Holy Spirit, let us pray for the common good of the whole human family.

FOR THE CHURCH
For God's holy church, gathered from every nation under heaven:
May we proclaim, in every language, God's mighty deeds of power.

FOR THE WORLD

For the United Nations and for all dedicated to world peace:
May the Spirit's power put an end to division and gather us as one.

FOR THOSE OPPRESSED, AFFLICTED OR IN NEED

For those excluded from the benefits enjoyed by the wider society:
May no earthly authority, and no fear of reprisal, repress their human rights.

FOR THE NEOPHYTES

For the neophytes who complete today the paschal season of mystagogy:
May they be faithful witnesses with us as members of the one body of Christ.

FOR THE NEEDS OF THE LOCAL COMMUNITY

For those whose labor is difficult, for those whose hearts are closed,
for those who are bereaved and for those who have gone astray:
May the Spirit comfort and heal, cleanse and restore.

For those who serve this community in a wide variety of ministries:
May the Spirit inspire all of us to place the gifts we have received at the service of the common good.

FOR THE CHRISTIAN ASSEMBLY

For this eucharistic assembly, as we conclude the season of paschal joy:
May the Spirit send us forth as witnesses to peace and reconciliation.

FOR THE DEAD

For those members of Christ's body, gone before us in death (especially N.):
May they receive virtue's sure reward and joys that never end.

Introduction to the Lord's Prayer

Because in Christ we have received the Spirit of adoption,
as sons and daughters of God we dare to pray:

Invitation to Holy Communion

Alleluia! Christ our paschal lamb has been sacrificed. Therefore, let us keep the festival.
Blessed are those who are called to the banquet of the Lamb.

Dismissal

Go forth in the power of the Spirit,
proclaiming the good news of Christ to all, Alleluia, Alleluia!

SECOND SUNDAY IN ORDINARY TIME
SECOND SUNDAY AFTER THE EPIPHANY

God of mystery,
whose voice whispers our name,
God in our midst,
whose Lamb walks among us unknown,
in every generation you reveal yourself
to those who long to know your dwelling place.

Speak now, Lord, for your servants are listening.
Draw us to you that with you we may always remain.

We ask this through our Lord Jesus Christ, your Son,
who lives and reigns with you
in the unity of the Holy Spirit,
God for ever and ever.

O God,
you reveal the signs of your presence among us
in the church, in the liturgy and in our brothers
    and sisters.
Let no word of yours ever fall by the wayside
or be rendered ineffective
through our indifference or neglect.
Rather, make us quick to recognize your saving plan
whenever we encounter it,
and keep us ready always
to serve as prophets and apostles of your kingdom.

We ask this through our Lord Jesus Christ, your Son,
who lives and reigns with you
in the unity of the Holy Spirit,
God for ever and ever.

Roman Lectionary	**Revised Common Lectionary**
1 Samuel 3:3b–10, 19	1 Samuel 3:1–10, (11–20)
Psalm 40:2, 4, 7–8, 10	Psalm 139:1–6, 13–18
1 Corinthians 6:13c–15a, 17–20	1 Corinthians 6:12–20
John 1:35–42	John 1:43–51

General Intercessions

Gathered at prayer in the temple of the Lord,
let us offer our intercession to the God who has called us by name.

FOR THE CHURCH
That the church may listen attentively to the voice of the Lord
and respond with courage and resourcefulness in God's service.

That Pope N., called to exercise the ministry of Peter in God's church,
may inspire by his own example our eager and ready response to Christ.

FOR THE WORLD
That the leaders of nations may hear in the voices of their people
God's own voice summoning the world to a future of justice and peace.

FOR THOSE OPPRESSED, AFFLICTED OR IN NEED

That those who are seeking meaning and purpose for their lives
may "come and see" and find in Christ the teacher for whom they search.

FOR THE NEEDS OF THE LOCAL COMMUNITY

That the married couples of our community
may be blessed by God with deepening love and steadfast fidelity.

That educators may inspire our young people
to embrace the beauty of chastity and develop relationships marked by mutual respect.

That the catechumens who have come to acknowledge Jesus as Messiah
may stay with us as we learn together from this anointed teacher.

That we who have heard the good news and followed Jesus
may find others who are in search of truth and bring them to Jesus.

FOR THE CHRISTIAN ASSEMBLY

That the Lord who speaks in this assembly
may find us to be servants who listen to God's voice and who delight to do God's will.

FOR THE DEAD

That those whom God has called to eternal life (especially N.)
may rejoice to remain forever with the Teacher they followed on earth

Introduction to the Lord's Prayer

Taught by our Savior's command and formed by the word of God,
we dare to pray:

Invitation to Holy Communion

Behold the Lamb of God, who takes away the sin of the world.
Blessed are those who are called to the banquet of the Lamb.

Dismissal

Listening for God's voice and eager to do God's will,
go in peace to love and serve the Lord.

THIRD SUNDAY IN ORDINARY TIME
THIRD SUNDAY AFTER THE EPIPHANY

The time is fulfilled, O God,
your kingdom comes near
and Christ bids us follow
and join in your work of compassion.

Let this call move our hearts and kindle our spirits,
so that, leaving other paths and gods,
we may follow where Jesus leads
and proclaim the good news of the kingdom
where this Christ lives and reigns with you
in the unity of the Holy Spirit,
God for ever and ever.

In your Son, O God, you have given us
your word in all its fullness
and the greatest of all your gifts.
Rouse our hearts to grasp the urgent need
   of conversion,
and stir up our souls with longing to embrace
   your gospel.
May our lives proclaim to those far away from you
and to those filled with doubt
that the one Savior of us all is your Son, our Lord
   Jesus Christ,
who lives and reigns with you
in the unity of the Holy Spirit,
God for ever and ever.

Roman Lectionary	**Revised Common Lectionary**
Jonah 3:1– 5, 10	Jonah 3:1– 5, 10
Psalm 25: 4 – 9	Psalm 62:5 –12
1 Corinthians 7:29 – 31	1 Corinthians 7:29 – 31
Mark 1:14 – 20	Mark 1:14 – 20

General Intercessions

In the name of Jesus, let us pray to God,
whose kingdom has come near.

FOR THE CHURCH
For the church, called like Jonah to preach God's word:
May it faithfully proclaim to the world the challenge of conversion.

FOR THE WORLD
For those consumed by work and possessions:
May they realize that the appointed time is short and use it to grow in love.

For all whose sins have alienated them from God:
May God stir them to repentance and set aside the threat of punishment.

For those who, like the first disciples, make their living from the water:
May God prosper their labor and bring them to safe harbor.

FOR THE NEEDS OF THE LOCAL COMMUNITY
For those whom God calls to serve in ministry:
May they respond eagerly as followers of Christ and fishers of people.

For those engaged in business and finance:
May they bear witness to Christ by their integrity and concern for the needy.

FOR THE CHRISTIAN ASSEMBLY
For this eucharistic assembly:
May our lives bear witness to our repentance and belief in the good news.

FOR THE DEAD
For those who have passed beyond this present world (especially N.):
May they live in the fullness of God's time and the joy of God's kingdom.

Introduction to the Lord's Prayer

Let us pray for the coming of the kingdom as Jesus taught us:

Invitation to Holy Communion

Behold the Lamb of God, who takes away the sin of the world.
Blessed are those who are called to the banquet of the Lamb.

Dismissal

Eager to follow Christ and to proclaim the nearness of God's kingdom,
go in peace to love and serve the Lord.

FOURTH SUNDAY IN ORDINARY TIME
FOURTH SUNDAY AFTER THE EPIPHANY

As one having authority, O God,
your Holy One comes to teach in this assembly
and to set our spirits free.

Release our hearts from all that binds us,
that with single-hearted resolve
and unhindered devotion,
the work of your kingdom
may claim all our energy and zeal.

We ask this through our Lord Jesus Christ, your Son,
who lives and reigns with you
in the unity of the Holy Spirit,
God for ever and ever.

In Christ your Son, O God, you impart to us
a new teaching from one who speaks with authority,
for Jesus is the unique master of wisdom,
and our only liberator from the forces of evil.
Make us convinced and courageous
    in professing our faith,
so that by word and deed we may proclaim the truth
and bear witness to the happiness enjoyed by those
who center their lives and put all their trust in you.

We ask this through our Lord Jesus Christ, your Son,
who lives and reigns with you
in the unity of the Holy Spirit,
God for ever and ever.

Roman Lectionary
Deuteronomy 18:15 – 20
Psalm 95: 1 – 2, 6 – 9
1 Corinthians 7:32 – 35
(Canada: 1 Corinthians 7:17, 32 – 35)
Mark 1:21 – 28

Revised Common Lectionary
Deuteronomy 18:15 – 20
Psalm 111
1 Corinthians 8:1 – 13
Mark 1:21 – 28

General Intercessions

Let us intercede for our own needs and the needs of all
in the name of Jesus of Nazareth, the Holy One of God.

FOR THE CHURCH
That the church may teach the truth of God
with an authority born of faithful witness and loving service.

FOR THE WORLD
That Jesus' teaching may rebuke the unclean spirits that torment our world:
greed and violence, oppression and despair.

That the Lord our God may raise up prophets in every land
and put in their mouths the challenging words of justice and peace.

That those burdened by emotional anguish or mental illness
may receive the care they need, the love they desire, the healing they seek.

FOR THE NEEDS OF THE LOCAL COMMUNITY
That those committed to celibacy for the sake of the gospel
may grow in holiness and joy through their service of God and neighbor.

That unmarried people may find happiness in the gift of friendship
and fulfillment in the kindness and care they extend to others.

That married couples may grow together in selfless love
and share the blessings of that love with the wider community.

That the catechumens may experience a spiritual liberation
from all that might deter them from following Jesus of Nazareth.

That each of us, leading the life to which God has called us,
may strive to support one another in love.

FOR THE CHRISTIAN ASSEMBLY
That we may heed the Lord who teaches us in this assembly
and spread the Lord's name by the sincerity of our witness.

FOR THE DEAD
That, with every unclean spirit cast out,
the faithful departed (especially N.) may be led into the presence of the Holy One of God.

Introduction to the Lord's Prayer

Taught by our Savior's command and formed by the word of God, we dare to pray:

Invitation to Holy Communion

Behold the Lamb of God, who takes away the sin of the world.
Blessed are those who are called to the banquet of the Lamb.

Dismissal

Listening for God's voice and eager to do God's will,
go in peace to love and serve the Lord.

FIFTH SUNDAY IN ORDINARY TIME

FIFTH SUNDAY AFTER THE EPIPHANY

To this house, O God,
the Teacher comes to preach and to heal.
Life's emptiness is filled, its misery transformed.

Lift us up from self-concern
and set us free for service to others.
May we go forth renewed and refreshed
to proclaim the good news.

We ask this through our Lord Jesus Christ, your Son,
who lives and reigns with you
in the unity of the Holy Spirit,
God for ever and ever.

With a father's care and a mother's compassion,
you embrace as your own, O good and loving God,
the sufferings borne by the whole human race,
and you join these to all that your Son endured
in his Passover from death's bitter pain to risen life.
In all our time of trial and testing,
purify our hearts and fortify us deep within,
so that, bearing the light of unfailing trust
in your power to heal and save,
we may hasten to the support of our brothers
   and sisters
as they face the mystery of illness and pain.

We ask this through our Lord Jesus Christ, your Son,
who lives and reigns with you
in the unity of the Holy Spirit,
God for ever and ever.

Roman Lectionary
Job 7:1–4, 6–7
Psalm 147:1–6
1 Corinthians 9:16–19, 22–23
Mark 1:29–39

Revised Common Lectionary
Isaiah 40:21–31
Psalm 147:1–11, 20c
1 Corinthians 9:16–23
Mark 1:29–39

General Intercessions

Let us join together in prayer to the God of compassion,
who heals the brokenhearted and binds up their wounds.

> **FOR THE CHURCH**
> That by proclaiming the message of God's healing love,
> Christians may help cast out the demons of prejudice and misunderstanding.

> **FOR THE WORLD**
> That by making themselves servants to all,
> world leaders may promote that human dignity that is rightfully due to all.

That those sick with various diseases of body, mind or spirit
may find Christ's healing at the hands of those who assist in their recovery.

That those burdened by anxious days and sleepless nights
may find comfort in their trials and direction for the future.

That those whose labor is hard and whose wages are inadequate
may receive the sustenance they need and work worthy of their dignity.

FOR THE NEEDS OF THE LOCAL COMMUNITY
That those called to our parish ministries
may be effective instruments of God's saving purpose.

FOR THE CHRISTIAN ASSEMBLY
That we whom Christ has lifted up to new life
may use the healing bestowed on us in the generous service of others.

FOR THE DEAD
That those who have passed through the long night of suffering and death (especially N.)
may come quickly to the dawn of eternal life in God's presence.

Introduction to the Lord's Prayer

Let us pray for the coming of the kingdom as Jesus taught us:

Invitation to Holy Communion

Behold the Lamb of God, who takes away the sin of the world.
Blessed are those who are called to the banquet of the Lamb.

Dismissal

Eager to follow Christ and to proclaim the nearness of God's kingdom,
go in peace to love and serve the Lord.

SIXTH SUNDAY IN ORDINARY TIME

SIXTH SUNDAY AFTER THE EPIPHANY
PROPER 1

In Jesus you stretch out your hand, O God,
to touch the unclean,
to love the unlovely
and to draw even the most despised and excluded
into the circle of your beloved disciples and friends.

Embraced by such love,
make us eager to heal others,
glad to herald a Savior whose kingdom includes all.

We ask this through our Lord Jesus Christ, your Son,
who lives and reigns with you
in the unity of the Holy Spirit,
God for ever and ever.

Cleanse and restore us, O God,
and heal us continually
from the sinfulness that divides us
and from the prejudice and discrimination
by which we degrade ourselves
    and dishonor your image in others.
Help us to stretch out our hands in love
especially to those our society scorns
and to recognize in their faces
the very image of Christ, blood-stained on
    the cross.
Thus may we take our part in your work of redemption
and proclaim to all
the wonders of your tender mercy and steadfast love.

We ask this through our Lord Jesus Christ, your Son,
who lives and reigns with you
in the unity of the Holy Spirit,
God for ever and ever.

Roman Lectionary
Leviticus 13:1–2, 44–46
Psalm 32:1–2, 5, 11
1 Corinthians 10:31—11:1
Mark 1:40–45

Revised Common Lectionary
2 Kings 5:1–14
Psalm 30
1 Corinthians 9:24–27
Mark 1:40–45
If this is the Sunday before Ash Wednesday, the following readings may be used in churches using Transfiguration readings on this day. Appropriate prayers may be found on page 158.
2 Kings 2:1–12
2 Corinthians 4:3–6
Psalm 50:1–6
Mark 9:2–9

General Intercessions

Seeking God's blessings not for ourselves only but for all,
let us pray to the God of steadfast love.

FOR THE CHURCH

For the church of God:
May its preaching and witness form consciences attuned to the glory of God and the dignity of others.

FOR THE WORLD

For this world in which so many suffer:
May the resources of health and healing be more equitably shared.

FOR THOSE OPPRESSED, AFFLICTED OR IN NEED

For all whom society stigmatizes as unclean:
May they know the hand of friendship and the touch of healing offered by Christians.

FOR THE NEEDS OF THE LOCAL COMMUNITY

For those engaged in medical research:
May their commitment to their discipline be enhanced by their compassion for the suffering.

For advocates who serve those whom society forces to live apart:
May their zeal and integrity move the hearts of others to conversion and concern.

For those who minister as physicians of the spirit: May they be instruments of God's peace
to all whose consciences are troubled or whose hearts are anxious.

For the sick of our community (especially N.): May Jesus stretch out his hand
and touch them with the healing power of grace and the presence of human compassion.

FOR THE CHRISTIAN ASSEMBLY

For us who eat and drink with the Lord at this eucharist:
May we do all for the glory of God and the good of our neighbor.

FOR THE DEAD

For the faithful departed (especially N.): May they be cleansed of every defilement
and come with joy into the presence of our high priest, Jesus Christ.

Introduction to the Lord's Prayer

Let us pray for the coming of the kingdom as Jesus taught us:

Invitation to Holy Communion

Behold the Lamb of God, who takes away the sin of the world.
Blessed are those who are called to the banquet of the Lamb.

Dismissal

Eager to follow Christ and to proclaim the nearness of God's kingdom,
go in peace to love and serve the Lord.

SEVENTH SUNDAY IN ORDINARY TIME

SEVENTH SUNDAY AFTER THE EPIPHANY
PROPER 2

God of new beginnings,

whose rivers make the desert blossom,

whose forgiveness reverses sin's power to cripple us.

Raise us up to stand strong

with people of faith in every generation,

that we may extend to others

the healing forgiveness we ourselves have received.

We ask this through our Lord Jesus Christ, your Son,

who lives and reigns with you

in the unity of the Holy Spirit,

God for ever and ever.

O God, whose will for each of us

is freedom of spirit and abiding peace deep in
   our hearts,

your gift of the forgiveness of sins is the living sign

that even now you are making the whole
   creation new.

In your love, reconcile us completely to yourself,

so our very lives may become

a living canticle of praise to your glory

and a living proclamation of the gospel of your mercy.

We ask this through our Lord Jesus Christ, your Son,

who lives and reigns with you

in the unity of the Holy Spirit,

God for ever and ever.

Roman Lectionary

Isaiah 43:18–19, 21–22, 24–25

Psalm 41:2–5, 13–14

2 Corinthians 1:18–22

Mark 2:1–12

Revised Common Lectionary

Isaiah 43:18–25

Psalm 41

2 Corinthians 1:18–22

Mark 2:1–12

If this is the Sunday before Ash Wednesday, the following readings may be used in churches using Transfiguration readings on this day. Appropriate prayers may be found on page 158.

2 Kings 2:1–12

2 Corinthians 4:3–6

Psalm 50:1–6

Mark 9:2–9

General Intercessions

Let us bring our intercessions before God,

who is making all things new.

FOR THE CHURCH

That the church's gospel message may be water in the desert and a way in the wilderness
for all who seek meaning and purpose in life.

That the memories of former conflicts and old hatreds may fade
as new beginnings of peace spring forth among the nations.

FOR THOSE OPPRESSED, AFFLICTED OR IN NEED

That those burdened by their own sins or wearied by the iniquity of others
may find in Christ the strength to rise up and continue on.

FOR THE NEEDS OF THE LOCAL COMMUNITY

That those with physical handicaps and those who are currently physically able
may enrich each other in mutual service.

That this community may grow in its sensitivity and service
to those kept apart from us by physical or emotional impairment.

That our parish may reach out to those who are alienated from the church,
offering them reconciliation and seeking their forgiveness for past hurts.

That those who are sick or homebound (especially N.)
may know their bond with us through our faithful visits and their sharing in our eucharist.

FOR THE CHRISTIAN ASSEMBLY

That we who are anointed and sealed with the gift of the Spirit
may always say "Yes" to God's promises and "Amen" to God's glory.

FOR THE DEAD

That, with their sins forgiven, our departed brothers and sisters (especially N.)
may rise in Christ and enter the home God has prepared for them.

Introduction to the Lord's Prayer

Let us pray for the coming of the kingdom as Jesus taught us:

Invitation to Holy Communion

Behold the Lamb of God, who takes away the sin of the world.
Blessed are those who are called to the banquet of the Lamb.

Dismissal

Eager to follow Christ and to proclaim the nearness of God's kingdom,
go in peace to love and serve the Lord.

EIGHTH SUNDAY IN ORDINARY TIME

EIGHTH SUNDAY AFTER THE EPIPHANY
PROPER 3

Into the wilderness you beckon us, O God,
speaking tenderly to our hearts,
coaxing us to respond with youthful fervor
to your covenant of faithful love.

At this feast where heaven and earth are wed,
clothe your poor with the garment of salvation
and quench our thirst with the new wine
   of your kingdom.

We ask this through our Lord Jesus Christ, your Son,
who lives and reigns with you
in the unity of the Holy Spirit,
God for ever and ever.

O God,
in Christ who is both Lord and Bridegroom
you invite the entire human race
to enter a new and everlasting covenant of love.
Whenever your church gathers for the eucharist,
may everyone recognize in our celebration
a joyful foretaste of the wedding banquet of the Lamb
and savor with us the joy of the gospel's new wine.

We ask this through our Lord Jesus Christ, your Son,
who lives and reigns with you
in the unity of the Holy Spirit,
God for ever and ever.

Roman Lectionary
Hosea 2:16, 17, 21–22
Psalm 103:1–4, 8, 10, 12–13
2 Corinthians 3:1–6
Mark 2:18–22

Revised Common Lectionary
Hosea 2:14–20
Psalm 103:1–13, 22
2 Corinthians 3:1–6
Mark 2:13–22
If this is the Sunday before Ash Wednesday, the following readings may be used in churches using Transfiguration readings on this day. Appropriate prayers may be found on page 158.
2 Kings 2:1–12
2 Corinthians 4:3–6
Psalm 50:1–6
Mark 9:2–9

General Intercessions

Invited by Jesus to be guests at this holy banquet,
let us lift up our needs in prayer before God whose compassion embraces all.

    FOR THE CHURCH
    For the people of God:
    May we listen to the Lord who speaks tenderly to us
    and respond with the faithfulness that marked the church's life in its youth.

For all nations, their leaders and citizens:
May a rebirth of love and mercy signal a new marriage of justice and peace.

FOR THOSE OPPRESSED, AFFLICTED OR IN NEED
For those who work for a just distribution of the world's food resources:
May their efforts reflect the generosity of Christ who invites all to his feast.

FOR THE NEEDS OF THE LOCAL COMMUNITY
For the married couples of our community:
May their faithfulness to each other mirror Christ's love for the church and God's steadfast love for
    all people.

For all who are ministers of the new covenant:
May they claim no honor for themselves but seek only to serve in the Spirit.

For our community's sick and homebound (especially N.):
May the new wine of restored health restore their youthfulness and joy.

FOR THE CHRISTIAN ASSEMBLY
For all of us gathered at the wedding banquet of the Lamb:
May our feasting proclaim our faith in Christ's abiding presence among us
and our fasting express our longing for the day of Christ's glorious return.

FOR THE DEAD
For those who have died (especially N.):
May God who is faithful take them to himself forever in steadfast love and mercy.

Introduction to the Lord's Prayer

Let us pray for the coming of the kingdom as Jesus taught us:

Invitation to Holy Communion

Behold the Lamb of God, who takes away the sin of the world.
Blessed are those who are called to the banquet of the Lamb.

Dismissal

Eager to follow Christ and to proclaim the nearness of God's kingdom,
go in peace to love and serve the Lord.

NINTH SUNDAY IN ORDINARY TIME

NINTH SUNDAY AFTER THE EPIPHANY
PROPER 4

Holy is this day, O Lord our God,
which you have made for celebration.
We glory in the beauty of the first creation
when you formed us in your image,
and in the new creation
when you raised us up in Christ.

We stretch out our hands to you:
Restore all that is withered within us
and renew your image in our lives.

We ask this through our Lord Jesus Christ, your Son,
who lives and reigns with you
in the unity of the Holy Spirit,
God for ever and ever.

O God,
in our weekly celebration of the Lord's Passover,
you illumine our hearts with the light of your glory
shining on the face of Christ Jesus.
Fill us with the power of your Spirit,
that we may enter a new and deeper relationship
with our brothers and sisters
and, indeed, with your whole creation.
Make us witnesses to the truth that sets us free,
and help us to become ministers of your freedom
   to all.

We ask this through our Lord Jesus Christ, your Son,
who lives and reigns with you
in the unity of the Holy Spirit,
God for ever and ever.

Roman Lectionary
Deuteronomy 5:12–15
Psalm 81:3–8, 10–11
2 Corinthians 4:6–11
Mark 2:23 — 3:6

Revised Common Lectionary
Deuteronomy 5:12–15
Psalm 81:1–10
2 Corinthians 4:5–12
Mark 2:23 — 3:6
If this is the Sunday before Ash Wednesday, the following readings are used in churches where this is Transfiguration Sunday. Appropriate prayers may be found on page 158.
2 Kings 2:1–12
2 Corinthians 4:3–6
Psalm 50:1–6
Mark 9:2–9

General Intercessions

On this day that the Lord has made his own,
let our prayers of intercession attend to the needs of all.

FOR THE CHURCH
That Christians may sanctify the Lord's Day
by offering living worship, enjoying restful leisure and renewing the bonds of family and friendship.

That the peoples of earth may not grieve the Lord by the hardness of their hearts
but permit God to restore withered hearts and hands to the work of peace.

FOR THOSE OPPRESSED, AFFLICTED OR IN NEED
That all enslaved by legalism may be set free
to find in the law of charity the supreme expression of fidelity to God and the covenant.

That refugees to our land may find in the hearts of believers
the hospitality and welcome we all hope to find in the heart of a loving God.

That those perplexed by life's difficulties may not despair
and those struck down may find Christian hands outstretched to lift them.

FOR THE NEEDS OF THE LOCAL COMMUNITY
That those who by sickness carry in their bodies the death of Jesus (especially N.)
may experience also the life of Christ within them.

That those whose day of rest is consumed by obligations to loved ones
may find comfort in the appreciation of those they serve.

FOR THE CHRISTIAN ASSEMBLY
That we may always come to the Lord's Day with hearts open
to receive the challenge of God's word and the healing power of Christ's touch.

FOR THE DEAD
That with a mighty hand and an outstretched arm
the Lord our God may bring the faithful departed (especially N.) into the promised land.

Introduction to the Lord's Prayer

Let us pray for the coming of the kingdom as Jesus taught us:

Invitation to Holy Communion

Behold the Lamb of God, who takes away the sin of the world.
Blessed are those who are called to the banquet of the Lamb.

Dismissal

Eager to follow Christ and to proclaim the nearness of God's kingdom,
go in peace to love and serve the Lord.

TENTH SUNDAY IN ORDINARY TIME

PROPER 5

Creator God,
we are fashioned, male and female,
in the likeness of your glory.

Gather us around Christ, our teacher.
Grant that by doing your will
we may truly become disciples,
brothers and sisters of the Son
who lives and reigns with you
in the unity of the Holy Spirit,
God for ever and ever.

You sent your Son, O God of our salvation,
to rescue us from the bondage of Satan
and to form us into the family of your people.
Arm us with the mighty weapons of faith,
the unfailing power of hope
and the unconquerable force of love,
that in our daily struggle against the Evil One
we may always share in the paschal victory of Christ.

We ask this through our Lord Jesus Christ, your Son,
who lives and reigns with you
in the unity of the Holy Spirit,
God for ever and ever.

Roman Lectionary
Genesis 3:9–15
Psalm 130:1–8
2 Corinthians 4:13 — 5:1
Mark 3:20–35

Revised Common Lectionary
1 Samuel 8:4–11, (12–15), 16–20, (11:14–15)
Psalm 138
or
Genesis 3:8–15
Psalm 130
2 Corinthians 4:13 — 5:1
Mark 3:20–35

General Intercessions

Welcomed into the family Christ has established by the gospel,
let us intercede in a spirit of faith for the needs of all.

FOR THE CHURCH
For all who gather around Jesus as their one teacher:
By doing the will of God may Christians be counted among the brothers and sisters of Christ.

FOR THE WORLD
For nations seduced by the attractions of wealth and power:
May selfish desires yield to a willingness to work together for peace.

FOR THOSE OPPRESSED, AFFLICTED OR IN NEED

For those who have lost heart beneath burdens of unemployment or homelessness:
May they be renewed day by day through the kindness and care of others.

For those whose motives are misjudged or whose reputations are maligned:
May truth prevail and goodness triumph over every misunderstanding.

For an end to domestic violence, ethnic hatred and racial prejudice:
May the goodness of Christ's gospel drive out the power of evil.

FOR THE NEEDS OF THE LOCAL COMMUNITY

For those who serve this community in the ministry of catechesis:
May their word and witness help form our parish into a household of faith.

For those whose health has declined under the burden of illness or age (especially N.):
May they be renewed inwardly and never lose heart.

FOR THE CHRISTIAN ASSEMBLY

For this eucharistic assembly:
May we persevere in unity as a family of faith
who listens to the word of Jesus and does the will of God.

FOR THE DEAD

For our brothers and sisters who have died (especially N.):
May the One who raised the Lord Jesus raise them also and bring us with them into his presence.

Introduction to the Lord's Prayer

For the coming of God's kingdom with its power of healing and peace,
let us pray as Jesus taught the first disciples:

Invitation to Holy Communion

The holy gifts of God for the holy people of God:
Draw near with awe and faith, with praise and thanksgiving.

Dismissal

As disciples of the kingdom, urged on by the love of Christ,
go in peace to love and serve the Lord.

ELEVENTH SUNDAY IN ORDINARY TIME

PROPER 6

Like scattered seed, whose growth is slow but steady,
your kingdom is revealed, O God.
At first so small,
its harvest provides for all who hunger.

Turn to us who measure progress
by standards so different from your own.
Give us trust in your ways of planting,
patience with gentle nurturing,
until we come to rest in the great branches
    of the cross.

Grant this through our Lord Jesus Christ, your Son,
who lives and reigns with you
in the unity of the Holy Spirit,
God for ever and ever.

From your bountiful hand, O God,
you have sown generously in our hearts
the seed of your truth and your grace.
May we welcome with humility and confidence
what you sow in the soil of our lives
and cultivate its growth with the patience the
    gospel teaches,
trusting completely and knowing full well
that peace and justice increase in this world
every time your word bears fruit in our lives.

We ask this through our Lord Jesus Christ, your Son,
who lives and reigns with you
in the unity of the Holy Spirit,
God for ever and ever.

Roman Lectionary	Revised Common Lectionary
Ezekiel 17:22 – 24	1 Samuel 15:34 —16:13
Psalm 92:2 – 3, 13 –16	Psalm 20
2 Corinthians 5:6 –10	*or*
Mark 4:26 – 34	Ezekiel 17:22 – 24
	Psalm 92:1– 4, 12 –15
	2 Corinthians 5:6 –10, (11–13), 14 –17
	Mark 4:26 – 34

General Intercessions

Walking by faith, not by sight,
let us pray with confidence to God whose kingdom grows among us.

FOR THE CHURCH
For the church in all its communities, great and small:
May its harvest increase and its branches be large enough to shelter all.

FOR THE WORLD

For prosperous nations who have resources in abundance:
May they mirror the generosity of God by offering a portion of their wealth and a ready welcome
to the needy.

FOR THOSE OPPRESSED, AFFLICTED OR IN NEED

For those who sow the seed and nurture the fruits of the earth:
May God provide a bountiful harvest for all to share.

For the oppressed who hunger for recognition of their human dignity:
May God lift high the lowly and make justice flourish.

For missionaries who sow the seeds of God's kingdom in faraway lands:
May their preaching and example cultivate the fruits of faith, hope and love.

FOR THE NEEDS OF THE LOCAL COMMUNITY

For those who teach the young, feed the hungry or comfort the afflicted:
May God plant the kingdom among us through these varied ministries.

For those whom sickness keeps at home or for whom travel has been taken away (especially N.):
May God grant health and safety to all who are absent from us.

FOR THE CHRISTIAN ASSEMBLY

For all of us called to be part of the kingdom:
May we persevere in prayer and work, trusting the God who brings great things from small beginnings.

FOR THE DEAD

For those who are now at home with the Lord (especially N.):
May they find mercy before the judgment seat of Christ and receive the reward of their goodness.

Introduction to the Lord's Prayer

For the coming of God's kingdom with its power of healing and peace,
let us pray as Jesus taught the first disciples:

Invitation to Holy Communion

The holy gifts of God for the holy people of God:
Draw near with awe and faith, with praise and thanksgiving.

Dismissal

As disciples of the kingdom, urged on by the love of Christ,
go in peace to love and serve the Lord.

TWELFTH SUNDAY IN ORDINARY TIME

PROPER 7

God of the whirlwind,
at creation's dawn
you set the bounds of the sea
and stilled the raging of its waves.

God of the calm,
in Jesus the Teacher
you rebuked the wind
and set the sea at rest:

Calm our fears now.
Stir up our faith,
that we may gladly lend our hands
to your work of making the whole creation new!

Grant this through our Lord Jesus Christ, your Son,
who lives and reigns with you
in the unity of the Holy Spirit,
God for ever and ever.

Make firm, Lord God, the faith of your
    Christian people,
that success may not fill us with worldly pride
nor the storms of life lay us low.
Rather, whatever may befall,
teach us to recognize your quiet but calming presence
and to count on you as the unseen companion
who faithfully accompanies us throughout
    life's journey.

We ask this through our Lord Jesus Christ, your Son,
who lives and reigns with you
in the unity of the Holy Spirit,
God for ever and ever.

Roman Lectionary
Job 38:1, 8–11
(Canada: Job 38:1–4, 8–11)
Psalm 107:23–26, 28–31
2 Corinthians 5:14–17
Mark 4:35–41

Revised Common Lectionary
1 Samuel 17:(1a, 4–11, 19–23), 32–49
Psalm 9:9–20
or
Job 38:1–11
Psalm 107:1–3, 23–32
or
1 Samuel 17:57—18:5, 10–16
Psalm 133
2 Corinthians 6:1–13
Mark 4:35–41

General Intercessions

Let us offer our prayers on behalf of all
to the God whose mighty power earth and heaven obey.

FOR THE CHURCH

That Christians who have grown fearful or discouraged
may have faith in the Teacher who will not permit us to perish.

FOR THE WORLD

That nations battered by the raging storms of violent conflict
may come one day to rejoice again in the calm of peace.

FOR THOSE OPPRESSED, AFFLICTED OR IN NEED

That those whose livelihood depends on the sea
may prosper in their labors and be preserved from danger.

FOR THE NEEDS OF THE LOCAL COMMUNITY

That vacationers may see God's handiwork in the splendor of wind and sea,
and be renewed in spirit by their time of recreation.

That those who question God's presence or purpose in their lives
may find in us a loving support and in God's love an ultimate answer.

FOR THE CHRISTIAN ASSEMBLY

That we who are blest to have Jesus present in our midst
may be filled with awe for our Teacher and love for each other.

FOR THE DEAD

That those who have crossed with Jesus from this life to the other side (especially N.)
may become a new creation in Christ for all eternity.

Introduction to the Lord's Prayer

Taught by our Savior's command and formed by the word of God, we dare to pray:

◆

For the coming of God's kingdom with its power of healing and peace,
let us pray as Jesus taught the first disciples:

Invitation to Holy Communion

The holy gifts of God for the holy people of God:
Draw near with awe and faith, with praise and thanksgiving.

Dismissal

As disciples of the kingdom, urged on by the love of Christ,
go in peace to love and serve the Lord.

THIRTEENTH SUNDAY IN ORDINARY TIME
PROPER 8

In Christ, O God, your healing power
restores to health a weary world.

In the word spoken here,
Christ bids us rise up and live.

Cast out our fear and revive our faith.
Make us live each day
in the joy for which you fashioned us.

We ask this through our Lord Jesus Christ, your Son,
who lives and reigns with you
in the unity of the Holy Spirit,
God for ever and ever.

O God,
in the paschal mystery of Christ,
who became poor for our sake
and obedient even unto death on a cross,
you have chosen to enrich us with every good gift
and to give us a share in Christ's exalted life.
Let us fear neither the cost of discipleship
nor the inevitability of sharing in the cross
but gladly announce to all our brothers and sisters
the good news of life healed, restored and renewed.

We ask this through our Lord Jesus Christ, your Son,
who lives and reigns with you
in the unity of the Holy Spirit,
God for ever and ever.

Roman Lectionary
Wisdom 1:13–15; 2:23–24
Psalm 30:2, 4–6, 11–13
2 Corinthians 8:7, 9, 13–15
Mark 5:21–43

Revised Common Lectionary
2 Samuel 1:1, 17–27
Psalm 130
or
Wisdom of Solomon 1:13–15; 2:23–24
Lamentations 3:23–33 *or* Psalm 30
2 Corinthians 8:7–15
Mark 5:21–43

General Intercessions

Let us pray to God in whose image we are made
and who delights in the wholeness of all creation.

FOR THE CHURCH
That in the face of death and evil, Christians may not fear
but believe in the power and presence of Christ.

FOR THE WORLD
That threatened by the poison of war and terrorism,
people of good will may seek peace and reconciliation.

That world leaders may work to achieve a balance
in which nations with an abundance assist those that are in need.

FOR THOSE OPPRESSED, AFFLICTED OR IN NEED
That those suffering chronic illness or long-term disability
may persevere in their struggle for wellness and in their faith in Christ.

That those whose lives are dedicated to the care of sick children
may know that Jesus, the Divine Physician, goes with them in their labor.

That parents who have suffered the death of a child
may find comfort in Christ's promise of eternal life and consolation in the loving care
    of family and friends.

FOR THE NEEDS OF THE LOCAL COMMUNITY
That the sick of our community (especially N.)
may welcome the healing presence of Jesus in the visits of friends and in the bread of the eucharist.

That those who grieve over the loss of loved ones
may be strengthened by the support of friends and the love of Christ.

FOR THOSE OPPRESSED, AFFLICTED OR IN NEED
That we whom Jesus has taken by the hand and lifted from the death of sin
may find nourishment in the eucharist we are given to eat.

FOR THE DEAD
That God who created us for incorruption
may give the righteous who have died (especially N.) immortal life.

Introduction to the Lord's Prayer

Taught by our Savior's command and formed by the word of God, we dare to pray:

◆

For the coming of God's kingdom with its power of healing and peace,
let us pray as Jesus taught the first disciples:

Invitation to Holy Communion

The holy gifts of God for the holy people of God:
Draw near with awe and faith, with praise and thanksgiving.

Dismissal

As disciples of the kingdom, urged on by the love of Christ,
go in peace to love and serve the Lord.

FOURTEENTH SUNDAY IN ORDINARY TIME

PROPER 9

Is this not the carpenter, O God, the child of Mary,
whose wisdom echoes across the centuries
to shape our lives to your image?

Let no unbelief of ours
impede Christ's deeds of power here,
but make that power perfect in our weakness
by your all-sufficient grace.

We ask this through our Lord Jesus Christ, your Son,
who lives and reigns with you
in the unity of the Holy Spirit,
God for ever and ever.

Remove from before our eyes, O God,
the veil that hides your splendor,
and flood us with the light of your Holy Spirit,
that we may recognize your glory
shining in the humiliation of your Christ
and experience even in our own human weakness
the sufficiency of your grace
and the surpassing power of Christ's resurrection.

We ask this through our Lord Jesus Christ, your Son,
who lives and reigns with you
in the unity of the Holy Spirit,
God for ever and ever.

Roman Lectionary
Ezekiel 2:2–5
Psalm 123:1–4
2 Corinthians 12:7–10
Mark 6:1–6

Revised Common Lectionary
2 Samuel 5:1–5, 9–10
Psalm 48
or
Ezekiel 2:1–5
Psalm 123
2 Corinthians 12:2–10
Mark 6:1–13

General Intercessions

Let us pray to God whose voice has spoken to us
and appeal to the One whose grace is always sufficient for our needs.

FOR THE CHURCH
For God's holy church:
May we not be a rebellious house but listen well to the prophets among us.

FOR THE WORLD
For the world community:
May our unbelief not block God's desire to do deeds of power and peace.

FOR THOSE OPPRESSED, AFFLICTED OR IN NEED

For people in need of food, housing or medical care:
May those with resources to help not refuse to hear the cries of the poor.

For those discouraged by any weakness:
May God's grace be sufficient and God's power be made perfect in them.

For those who have grown cynical or skeptical:
May God give them new openness to wisdom, truth and goodness.

For those who are insulted or persecuted for the sake of conscience:
May God give them strength to persevere and courage in bearing witness.

FOR THE NEEDS OF THE LOCAL COMMUNITY

For those who work on behalf of social justice:
May their prophetic voices find a willing response from our community.

For those who pray that sickness or distress may leave them (especially N.):
May the power of Christ dwell in them and strengthen them.

FOR THE CHRISTIAN ASSEMBLY

For this eucharistic assembly:
May Jesus' teaching dispel our unbelief and his deeds of power heal us.

FOR THE DEAD

For those who honored Jesus by their living (especially N.):
May Jesus welcome them now into heaven, their true home.

Introduction to the Lord's Prayer

Taught by our Savior's command and formed by the word of God, we dare to pray:

◆

For the coming of God's kingdom with its power of healing and peace,
let us pray as Jesus taught the first disciples:

Invitation to Holy Communion

The holy gifts of God for the holy people of God:
Draw near with awe and faith, with praise and thanksgiving.

Dismissal

As disciples of the kingdom, urged on by the love of Christ,
go in peace to love and serve the Lord.

FIFTEENTH SUNDAY IN ORDINARY TIME
PROPER 10

O God of salvation,
you adopt us through Jesus Christ,
and you call us to proclaim the good news
of your healing power and forgiving love.

Give us an unfailing trust
that the wealth of your word is sufficient,
the food and drink you provide is ample.
Then send us out with praise on our lips.

We ask this through our Lord Jesus Christ, your Son,
who lives and reigns with you
in the unity of the Holy Spirit,
God for ever and ever.

Let nothing, O God, be dearer to us than your Son,
no worldly possessions, no human honors;
let us prefer nothing whatever to Christ,
who alone makes known to the world the mystery
   of your love
and reveals the true dignity of every human person.
Grant us only the riches of your grace,
and pour forth on us the full measure of your Spirit,
that by word and deed we may proclaim Christ,
in whom you bestow forgiveness and redemption
   on all.

We ask this through our Lord Jesus Christ, your Son,
who lives and reigns with you
in the unity of the Holy Spirit,
God for ever and ever.

Roman Lectionary
Amos 7:12–15
Psalm 85:9–14
Ephesians 1:3–10, (11–14)
Mark 6:7–13

Revised Common Lectionary
2 Samuel 6:1–5, 12b–19
Psalm 24
or
Amos 7:7–15
Psalm 85:8–13
Ephesians 1:3–14
Mark 6:14–29

General Intercessions

As a people redeemed and forgiven, let us earnestly pray to God,
who freely bestows the riches of grace on all in Christ the Beloved.

FOR THE CHURCH
That the church, sent by God for the healing of the nations,
may proclaim Christ with courage and conviction, in simplicity and service.

That God's people may not fear or silence prophetic voices
who challenge us to be more faithful to the gospel covenant.

FOR THE WORLD

That mutual acknowledgment and repentance for the conflicts of the past
may drive from our world the demons of war and heal the wounds of discord.

FOR THOSE OPPRESSED, AFFLICTED OR IN NEED

That missionaries may be sustained by active support from friends at home
and encouraged by a ready welcome in distant lands.

That those who confront our complacency by their words and example
may lead society to a conversion that fosters justice and dignity for all.

FOR THE NEEDS OF THE LOCAL COMMUNITY

That the sacrament of anointing and our community's compassion
may bring healing and strength to those who are sick (especially N.).

That we may cheerfully extend to vacationers and travelers
the hospitality of faith and the fellowship of our community.

That parents and children brought together by adoption may see in their relationship
a living image of God's adoption of each one of us in Christ Jesus.

FOR THE CHRISTIAN ASSEMBLY

That we who are redeemed in Christ's blood and forgiven our trespasses
may eagerly make known to all the mystery of God's saving love for them.

FOR THE DEAD

That those departed who believed in Christ and were sealed with the Holy Spirit (especially N.)
may now receive the promised inheritance of redemption.

Introduction to the Lord's Prayer

As teacher and healer, Jesus came to us from God.
Now for the world's salvation and God's glory, we pray as Jesus taught us:

Invitation to Holy Communion

Behold the Lamb of God, who takes away the sin of the world.
Blessed are those who are called to the banquet of the Lamb.

Dismissal

Sent in the name of Christ, whose compassion embraces all,
go in peace to love and serve the Lord.

SIXTEENTH SUNDAY IN ORDINARY TIME

PROPER 11

Lord God, faithful shepherd of the flock,
in Jesus you long to gather into one fold
the scattered sheep,
the desolate crowd,
the souls bewildered and confused.

Work in us and through us to fashion a new humanity,
proclaiming peace to those near and those far off,
gathering many into one through Christ's
    glorious cross.

We ask this through our Lord Jesus Christ, your Son,
who lives and reigns with you
in the unity of the Holy Spirit,
God for ever and ever.

As we gather again, O God,
to celebrate the weekly Pasch,
grant your church the joy of tasting again
the living presence of your Christ
in the word that is proclaimed
and in the bread of life we break.
Drawing apart on this day of worship and rest,
of refreshment and renewal,
let us recognize in Jesus
the true prophet and shepherd
who guides us to unfailing springs of eternal joy.

We ask this through our Lord Jesus Christ, your Son,
who lives and reigns with you
in the unity of the Holy Spirit,
God for ever and ever.

Roman Lectionary

Jeremiah 23:1–6
Psalm 23:1–6
Ephesians 2:13–18
Mark 6:30–34

Revised Common Lectionary

2 Samuel 7:1–14a
Psalm 89:20–37
or
Jeremiah 23:1–6
Psalm 23
Ephesians 2:11–22
Mark 6:30–34, 53–56

General Intercessions

As disciples gathered around Jesus,
let us offer to the Lord our intercessions for all God's children.

> FOR THE CHURCH
> For those called to shepherd the Lord's flock (especially N., our pope; N., our bishop;
>   and N., our pastor):
> May they attend with compassion to the needs of all.

FOR THE WORLD

For the birth of a new humanity, reconciled to God and to each other:
May Christ be our peace, putting to death the hostility that divides us.

For those who serve in the courts of law:
May they judge wisely and administer justice and righteousness in the land.

FOR THOSE OPPRESSED, AFFLICTED OR IN NEED

For those whom society has abandoned:
May Christians extend to them the compassion of Christ the Shepherd.

For an increase of understanding between Jews and Christians:
May the covenant's wisdom and Christ's gospel deepen our mutual respect.

FOR THE NEEDS OF THE LOCAL COMMUNITY

For those who work in law enforcement:
May their wisdom and responsibility enable the community to live in safety.

For those who encourage dialogue among diverse groups in this city (town):
May we see that beyond our divisions we are members of one body.

FOR THE CHRISTIAN ASSEMBLY

For us who have been brought near to God and to each other by the blood of Christ:
May we proclaim to all the peace God has bestowed on us.

FOR THE DEAD

For those the Good Shepherd has gathered to himself (especially N.):
May they live forever in the Lord's fold.

Introduction to the Lord's Prayer

As teacher and healer, Jesus came to us from God.
Now for the world's salvation and God's glory, we pray as Jesus taught us:

Invitation to Holy Communion

Behold the Lamb of God, who takes away the sin of the world.
Blessed are those who are called to the banquet of the Lamb.

Dismissal

Sent in the name of Christ, whose compassion embraces all,
go in peace to love and serve the Lord.

SEVENTEENTH SUNDAY IN ORDINARY TIME
PROPER 12

We lift our eyes to you, O God,
we stretch out our hands in supplication.

What you give we will share,
for you have made us one body in one Spirit.
Sustain with your word and food
all whom you have called to one hope,
and let nothing be lost of the community
that you have bound together in love and peace.

We ask this through our Lord Jesus Christ,
the living bread, who has come down from heaven
for the life of the world,
who lives and reigns with you and the Holy Spirit,
God for ever and ever.

In the Sunday Pasch, Lord God,
you call us to share with one another
the living bread that has come down from heaven.
Fill us with the charity of Christ
and stir us by his own example
to break the bread of earth as well
and to share it generously with others,
so that every hunger of body and spirit may be
satisfied.

We ask this through our Lord Jesus Christ, your Son,
who lives and reigns with you
in the unity of the Holy Spirit,
God for ever and ever.

Roman Lectionary
2 Kings 4:42–44
Psalm 145:10–11, 15–18
Ephesians 4:1–6
John 6:1–15

Revised Common Lectionary
2 Samuel 11:1–15
Psalm 14
or
2 Kings 4:42–44
Psalm 145:10–18
Ephesians 3:14–21
John 6:1–21

General Intercessions

Let us turn in prayer to God
who is near to those who call and whose bounty feeds all.

FOR THE CHURCH

That the church may be the instrument by which the bread of life is broken for those who hunger.

That all who are united by sharing one Lord, one faith, one baptism
may also be gathered into unity and fed by Jesus with the one bread of life.

That peoples of differing cultures may recognize our common humanity
and live a life that is worthy of the children of one God and Father.

That the more prosperous nations may work generously and in peace
for a just allocation of the food of the earth.

FOR THOSE OPPRESSED, AFFLICTED OR IN NEED
That those who hunger in body or spirit for life's necessities
may be fed by the hand of Jesus and by the ministry of Jesus' disciples.

That those in prison and all who minister to them in Christ's love
may experience the healing that flows from the one hope of our calling.

FOR THE NEEDS OF THE LOCAL COMMUNITY
That those who minister the bread of life to our sick and homebound
may be for them a living sign of Christ's concern and of our care.

That we may support those who prepare our young people for the eucharist
by the fervor of our worship and the fidelity of our witness.

That this community, nourished at the one table of the Lord,
may maintain the unity of the Spirit in the bond of peace.

FOR THE CHRISTIAN ASSEMBLY
That we who partake of the one bread may lead a life worthy of our calling,
patiently bearing with one another in love.

FOR THE DEAD
That those who were nourished in this life by the bread Jesus gives
may celebrate forever the paschal festival of the kingdom (especially N.).

Introduction to the Lord's Prayer

With trust in God whose providence nourishes and sustains us,
we pray now as Jesus taught us:

Invitation to Holy Communion

Behold the living bread come down from heaven: Those who eat of it will never die.
Behold the cup of eternal life: Those who drink of it will live forever.

Dismissal

In the strength of the living bread that Christ has given us,
go in peace to love and serve the Lord.

EIGHTEENTH SUNDAY IN ORDINARY TIME

PROPER 13

O God, whose gift to our ancestors
was manna in the wilderness,
we believe in the One whom you have sent,
on whom you have set your seal.

Nourish us on the bread of Christ's teaching,
clothe us in your likeness.
May we live a life worthy of our calling
and bear witness in true holiness.

We ask this through our Lord Jesus Christ,
the living bread, who has come down from heaven
    for the life of the world,
who lives and reigns with you and the Holy Spirit,
God for ever and ever.

To our stewardship, O God, you have entrusted
the vast resources of your creation.
Let there be no lack of bread
at the tables of any of your children,
and stir up within us also a longing for your word,
that we may be able to satisfy that hunger for truth
that you have placed within every human heart.

We ask this through our Lord Jesus Christ, your Son,
who lives and reigns with you
in the unity of the Holy Spirit,
God for ever and ever.

Roman Lectionary	Revised Common Lectionary
Exodus 16:2 – 4, 12 –15	2 Samuel 11:26 —12:13a
Psalm 78:3 – 4, 23 – 25, 54	Psalm 51:1–12
Ephesians 4:17, 20 – 24	*or*
John 6:24 – 35	Exodus 16:2 – 4, 9 –15
	Psalm 78:23 – 29
	Ephesians 4:1–16
	John 6:24 – 35

General Intercessions

To the good and gracious God who gives us bread from heaven,
let us join in heartfelt prayer on behalf of the needs of all.

FOR THE CHURCH
That the church, on its pilgrimage to the land of promise,
may never doubt God's providence but draw strength from the bread of life.

That all Christians, clothed in God's likeness,
may find unity in the bread from heaven that God has given them to eat.

FOR THE WORLD

That in a world where so many are afflicted by hunger,
nations may set aside differences and assume responsibility for each other.

FOR THOSE OPPRESSED, AFFLICTED OR IN NEED

That those for whom life has become a journey through the wilderness
may experience God's abiding care in the loving concern of God's servants.

That all who put aside their former way of life
may be renewed in mind and spirit, in true righteousness and holiness.

FOR THE NEEDS OF THE LOCAL COMMUNITY

That we who share the bread from heaven in our worship
may be inspired to provide daily bread for those who are in need.

That by our commitment to community projects on behalf of the needy
we may bear the witness of God's love to all who look for signs of hope.

FOR THE CHRISTIAN ASSEMBLY

That we may never become lost in pursuit of food that perishes
but learn from our worship to cherish the gifts that endure.

That we who feed on the bread of heaven may do the work of God
by believing in Christ and by living Christ's gospel.

FOR THE DEAD

That the departed who believed in Jesus in this life (especially N.)
may never be hungry or thirsty again.

Introduction to the Lord's Prayer

With trust in God, whose providence nourishes and sustains us,
we pray now as Jesus taught us:

Invitation to Holy Communion

Behold the living bread come down from heaven: Those who eat of it will never die.
Behold the cup of eternal life: Those who drink of it will live forever.

Dismissal

In the strength of the living bread that Christ has given us,
go in peace to love and serve the Lord.

NINETEENTH SUNDAY IN ORDINARY TIME

PROPER 14

By your angel's hand, O God, you gave Elijah bread
to be the food that sustained him
on the journey to your holy mountain.
In Jesus you give us the living bread
for the life of the world,
our food for the journey to your kingdom.

Forgiving one another as you have forgiven us,
let us come to that banquet of life immortal
of which our table here is foretaste and pledge.

We ask this through our Lord Jesus Christ,
the living bread, who has come down from heaven
    for the life of the world,
who lives and reigns with you and the Holy Spirit,
God for ever and ever.

Guide your church, O God,
on the paths of its earthly pilgrimage,
and sustain with the food that does not perish
so that, persevering in the faith
to which Christ has called us,
we may come at last to your holy mountain
and gaze on the beauty of your face.

We ask this through our Lord Jesus Christ, your Son,
who lives and reigns with you
in the unity of the Holy Spirit,
God for ever and ever.

Roman Lectionary	**Revised Common Lectionary**
1 Kings 19:4 – 8	2 Samuel 18:5 – 9, 15, 31 – 33
Psalm 34:2 – 9	Psalm 130
Ephesians 4:30 — 5:2	*or*
John 6:41 – 51	1 Kings 19:4 – 8
	Psalm 34:1 – 8
	Ephesians 4:25 — 5:2
	John 6:35, 41 – 51

General Intercessions

In prayer let us seek the Lord, who hears and responds to all.

FOR THE CHURCH
That the church may be sustained on its journey toward God's mountain
by the food that God so generously bestows.

That Christians may not grieve the Holy Spirit by our divisions
but come to share in unity of faith the one bread that comes from heaven.

FOR THE WORLD

That nations may put away bitterness and anger, slander and malice,
and be kind to one another, tenderhearted and forgiving.

That nations may not continue the discord of their ancestors
but be taught by God the vision of peace proclaimed by the prophets.

FOR THOSE OPPRESSED, AFFLICTED OR IN NEED

That those who in their despair seek to end their lives
may find new strength for life's journey from God and from believers.

That those who make and influence public policy may not subject the poor to slander
but seek to offer them society's kindness and care.

FOR THE NEEDS OF THE LOCAL COMMUNITY

That the hungry may find us to be angels of God's providence
who gladly provide the food and assistance to help them live and thrive.

That those wounded by the thoughtlessness or malice of others
may find the grace to forgive as God has forgiven us all in Christ.

FOR THE CHRISTIAN ASSEMBLY

That this assembly, fed with the living bread that comes down from heaven,
may bear witness in self-sacrificing love.

FOR THE DEAD

That believers who ate the bread from heaven in this life (especially N.)
may live forever as Christ promises.

Introduction to the Lord's Prayer

With trust in God whose providence nourishes and sustains us,
we pray now as Jesus taught us:

Invitation to Holy Communion

Behold the living bread come down from heaven: Those who eat of it will never die.
Behold the cup of eternal life: Those who drink of it will live forever.

Dismissal

In the strength of the living bread that Christ has given us,
go in peace to love and serve the Lord.

TWENTIETH SUNDAY IN ORDINARY TIME
PROPER 15

Here in our midst, O good and gracious God,
Wisdom has built herself a house,
she has set her table and mixed her wine:
The flesh and blood of Christ
become our food and drink.

Fill us with your Spirit,
with psalms and hymns and spiritual songs,
so that we may be a canticle of praise to you,
and for our brothers and sisters a feast of joyful love.

We ask this through our Lord Jesus Christ,
the living bread, who has come down from heaven
    for the life of the world,
who lives and reigns with you and the Holy Spirit,
God for ever and ever.

On this holy day, O God of life,
you have made us your friends
and have invited us to be guests at your table.
Behold your church assembled here,
and hear us who sing to you on our journey through
    this life
the psalms and hymns and spiritual songs
that proclaim our blessed hope of resurrection in the
    life to come.
Confirm our trust that we will share one day
in the banquet of your eternal kingdom.

We ask this through our Lord Jesus Christ, your Son,
who lives and reigns with you
in the unity of the Holy Spirit,
God for ever and ever.

Roman Lectionary
Proverbs 9:1–6
Psalm 34:2–3, 10–15
Ephesians 5:15–20
John 6:51–58

Revised Common Lectionary
1 Kings 2:10–12; 3:3–14
Psalm 111
or
Proverbs 9:1–6
Psalm 34:9–14
Ephesians 5:15–20
John 6:51–58

General Intercessions

Let us call on the living Father, whose Son has spoken the word of life
and whose wisdom has set her table.

FOR THE CHURCH

That the church may seek its strength not from worldly wealth and power
but from the true food and true drink the Lord alone provides.

That the church may be seen by the world as the house of wisdom,
where the simple are welcomed to share the feast of faith and charity.

FOR THE WORLD

That nations may look to Christ, the living bread, to satisfy their longing
for a peace that will last and for a justice that will never fail.

FOR THOSE OPPRESSED, AFFLICTED OR IN NEED

That all who hunger for the bread of freedom may find it in the gospel of Jesus,
in whom all ancient hungers are satisfied.

That those whose serenity is shaken by the turmoil of difficult days
may discover peace of mind as they come to understand the Lord's will.

FOR THE NEEDS OF THE LOCAL COMMUNITY

That God may inspire the music ministry of this community
as they help us make music to the Lord with our hearts and voices.

That those who share wisdom's many gifts within and beyond our parish
may nurture others and inspire them to walk in the way of insight.

FOR THE CHRISTIAN ASSEMBLY

That we who eat the flesh of the Son of Man and drink his blood
may mature in faith and have the very life of Christ within us.

That this eucharistic assembly may be filled with the Spirit and strengthened for witness
as we sing psalms, hymns and spiritual songs.

FOR THE DEAD

That those gone before us in faith who ate the bread of life on earth (especially N.)
may be raised up on the last day to live for ever.

Introduction to the Lord's Prayer

With trust in God whose providence nourishes and sustains us,
we pray now as Jesus taught us:

Invitation to Holy Communion

Behold the living bread come down from heaven: Those who eat of it will never die.
Behold the cup of eternal life: Those who drink of it will live forever.

Dismissal

In the strength of the living bread that Christ has given us,
go in peace to love and serve the Lord.

TWENTY-FIRST SUNDAY IN ORDINARY TIME

PROPER 16

In Jesus, your Holy One,
you have given us the words of eternal life, O God,
but you leave your household free to choose
whom we will serve:
the gods of the lands in which we live,
or you, the living God.

Far be it from us to forsake you!
To whom else can we go?
Nourish us with Christ's flesh and blood.
May we have life ourselves,
and bring life-giving love to others.

We ask this through our Lord Jesus Christ,
the living bread, who has come down from heaven
    for the life of the world,
who lives and reigns with you and the Holy Spirit,
God for ever and ever.

God our Savior,
in Christ, your eternal Word,
you have revealed the full depths of your love for us.
Guide this holy assembly of your people
by the light of your Holy Spirit,
so that no word of mere human wisdom
may ever cause us to turn away from your Holy One,
the Lord, who alone has the words of eternal life,
and who lives and reigns with you
in the unity of the Holy Spirit,
God for ever and ever.

Roman Lectionary
Joshua 24:1–2a, 15–17, 18b
Psalm 34:2–3, 16–23
Ephesians 5:(21–24), 25–32
(Canada: Ephesians 4:32 — 5:2, 21–32)
John 6:60–69

Revised Common Lectionary
1 Kings 8:(1, 6, 10–11), 22–30
Psalm 84
or
Joshua 24:1–2a, 14–18
Psalm 34:15–22
Ephesians 6:10–20
John 6:56–69

General Intercessions

Let this household of faith present itself now before the Lord our God,
praying to the One whose mighty deeds are known to all.

FOR THE CHURCH

That Christians may reject the values of society that contradict the gospel
and choose to serve the Lord whose gifts are freedom and fidelity.

That the difficult teachings of Jesus may not discourage Christians
but challenge us to ask for the grace to embrace the cost of discipleship.

That God may deliver our world from its slavery to violence
and set the nations free to pursue reconciliation and peace.

That those on whom society has turned its back may not despair
but be comforted to find that Christ's disciples will not abandon them.

That women may be able to share their talents in church and society
and that these communities may welcome the gifts and challenges they bring.

That our catechumens and all who have not yet shared the eucharist
may persevere until they are one with us at this table.

That the wives and husbands of our community may grow in love
and be living signs of Christ's love for the church.

That those whose faith is tested may not walk away
but stay near Christ who has the words of eternal life.

That this assembly may find Christ's words to be spirit and life
and Christ's flesh and blood to be the source of life within us.

That we, who have come to know and believe in Christ as God's Holy One
may imitate Christ by serving one another in reverence and humility.

That those who served God and remained loyal to Christ in this life (especially N.)
may see Christ, who has ascended to where he was before.

Introduction to the Lord's Prayer

With trust in God whose providence nourishes and sustains us,
we pray now as Jesus taught us:

Invitation to Holy Communion

Behold the living bread come down from heaven: Those who eat of it will never die.
Behold the cup of eternal life: Those who drink of it will live forever.

Dismissal

In the strength of the living bread that Christ has given us,
go in peace to love and serve the Lord.

TWENTY-SECOND SUNDAY IN ORDINARY TIME

PROPER 17

Lord God of our ancestors,
whose statutes and ordinances
are for all time a way of holiness,
cleanse us through and through,
and keep our hearts faithful.

As we welcome your saving word,
help us speak it in the generous service
of those most in need,
for this alone is religion pure and undefiled.

We ask this through our Lord Jesus Christ, your Son,
who lives and reigns with you
in the unity of the Holy Spirit,
God for ever and ever.

Behold, O God, your Christian people,
gathered together on this day of the Lord,
our weekly celebration of the Pasch of Christ.
Let the praise on our lips
resound in the depths of our hearts,
the word you have sown,
the word that has taken root within us
to sanctify and renew our entire lives.

We ask this through our Lord Jesus Christ, your Son,
who lives and reigns with you
in the unity of the Holy Spirit,
God for ever and ever.

Roman Lectionary
Deuteronomy 4:1–2, 6–8
Psalm 15:2–5
James 1:17–18, 21b–22, 27
Mark 7:1–8, 14–15, 21–23

Revised Common Lectionary
Song of Solomon 2:8–13
Psalm 45:1–2, 6–9
or
Deuteronomy 4:1–2, 6–9
Psalm 15
James 1:17–27
Mark 7:1–8, 14–15, 21–23

General Intercessions

Let us offer our prayer to the Lord, the God of our ancestors,
who is near to us whenever we call.

FOR THE CHURCH

For the church: May it grow in faithfulness to God's commandments,
interpreting them with wisdom and discernment for the holiness of all.

For those who hand on the tradition of the church (especially N., our pope; N., our bishop;
and N., our pastor):
May their teaching illumine God's covenant and draw our hearts to it.

For the world:
May all peoples know how close God is to those who live the law of love.

For the leaders of nations:
May the Lord purify their inmost hearts and direct their thoughts to peace.

FOR THOSE OPPRESSED, AFFLICTED OR IN NEED

For those in any need:
May all who honor God with their lips serve Christ, who suffers in others.

For all victims of the evils that come from the human heart:
May they find healing for their pain and hope for their future.

FOR THE NEEDS OF THE LOCAL COMMUNITY

For our parish community:
May avarice and pride, slander and deceit and every other defilement be far from our hearts.

For this faith community:
May we cherish unity in essentials, diversity in nonessentials and charity in all things.

FOR THE CHRISTIAN ASSEMBLY

For this eucharistic assembly:
May the worship of our lips be matched by the fidelity of our hearts.

For us who have assembled to keep holy the Lord's Day:
May we welcome and live the word that has the power to save our souls.

FOR THE DEAD

For the faithful departed (especially N.):
May they enter in and occupy the land that the Lord God has promised.

Introduction to the Lord's Prayer

As teacher and healer, Jesus came to us from God.
Now for the world's salvation and God's glory, we pray as Jesus taught us:

Invitation to Holy Communion

Behold the Lamb of God, who takes away the sin of the world.
Blessed are those who are called to the banquet of the Lamb.

Dismissal

Sent in the name of Christ, whose compassion embraces all,
go in peace to love and serve the Lord.

TWENTY-THIRD SUNDAY IN ORDINARY TIME

PROPER 18

Into the dry and thirsty wilderness of our world,
O strong and faithful God,
you come with streams of living water
to quench our thirst,
to cleanse our wounds,
to refresh our weary souls!

Open our eyes to your presence everywhere.
Unstop our ears to hear the challenge of your word.
Loose our tongues in songs of praise
and fearless witness to your justice.

We ask this through our Lord Jesus Christ, your Son,
who lives and reigns with you
in the unity of the Holy Spirit,
God for ever and ever.

O good and gracious God,
you have chosen little ones, the world's poor
and lowly,
to become rich in faith and to be heirs
of your kingdom.
Help us to speak words of encouragement and
strength to all whose hearts are fearful,
that the tongue of the speechless may be loosened
and all of our wounded humanity,
unable so much as to pray,
may join us in singing the mighty wonders
of your love.

We ask this through our Lord Jesus Christ, your Son,
who lives and reigns with you
in the unity of the Holy Spirit,
God for ever and ever.

Roman Lectionary
Isaiah 35:4 – 7a
Psalm 146:7 – 10
James 2:1 – 5
Mark 7:31 – 37

Revised Common Lectionary
Proverbs 22:1 – 2, 8 – 9, 22 – 23
Psalm 125
or
Isaiah 35:4 – 7a
Psalm 146
James 2:1 – 10, (11 – 13), 14 – 17
Mark 7:24 – 37

General Intercessions

For the needs of the whole world let us pray now to our God,
who comes with salvation to make us strong and cast out our fear.

FOR THE CHURCH
For God's holy church:
May it be an instrument of Christ's compassion and healing for all in need.

For the church's growth in authentic witness to Christ:
May its priorities mirror God's own preferential love for the poor.

FOR THE WORLD
For leaders of nations:
May they cooperate to advance world peace and to reduce anxiety and fear.

For those who control the world's resources:
May God turn their attention to the needs of the poor.

FOR THOSE OPPRESSED, AFFLICTED OR IN NEED
For victims of discrimination and prejudice:
May they be accorded the respect to which their human dignity is entitled.

FOR THE NEEDS OF THE LOCAL COMMUNITY
For our growth in sensitivity to those who are disabled:
May this community be in every way accessible to all who seek the Lord.

For all who work with the handicapped and for all those they serve:
May their care for each other be a source of mutual enrichment and joy.

FOR THE CHRISTIAN ASSEMBLY
For this assembly, gathered in the name of the glorious Lord Jesus:
May no one who comes among us experience discrimination or rejection.

FOR THE DEAD
For those who in life were members of this assembly (especially N.):
May they inherit the kingdom promised to those who love God.

Introduction to the Lord's Prayer

As teacher and healer, Jesus came to us from God.
Now for the world's salvation and God's glory, we pray as Jesus taught us:

Invitation to Holy Communion

Behold the Lamb of God, who takes away the sin of the world.
Blessed are those who are called to the banquet of the Lamb.

Dismissal

Sent in the name of Christ, whose compassion embraces all,
go in peace to love and serve the Lord.

TWENTY-FOURTH SUNDAY IN ORDINARY TIME
PROPER 19

Not in easy words, O God, but in selfless deeds
is the faith we profess made real
and the love our Master commanded made present.

Give us the strength to take up the cross and
wisdom to follow where Christ leads,
losing our lives for the sake of the gospel.

We ask this through our Lord Jesus Christ, your Son,
who lives and reigns with you
in the unity of the Holy Spirit,
God for ever and ever.

Lord God, the strength of your servants,
do not abandon us in our weakness and suffering,
but let your Holy Spirit come to our aid.
By our good works may we show forth our faith
that Jesus is indeed the Christ,
so that we may take up the cross and follow the Lord,
certain that we will save our lives
only when we have the courage to lose them
for the sake of Christ and for the sake of the gospel.

We ask this through our Lord Jesus Christ, your Son,
who lives and reigns with you
in the unity of the Holy Spirit,
God for ever and ever.

Roman Lectionary
Isaiah 50:4–9
Psalm 116:1–6, 8–9
James 2:14–18
Mark 8:27–35

Revised Common Lectionary
Proverbs 1:20–33
Psalm 19
or
Wisdom of Solomon 7:26 — 8:1
or
Isaiah 50:4–9a
Psalm 116:1–9
James 3:1–12
Mark 8:27–38

General Intercessions

To the Lord God who always helps us,
let us pray in the name of Jesus, God's servant.

FOR THE CHURCH
That all who confess Jesus as Messiah may take up the cross
and follow Jesus by sacrificing themselves for the sake of the gospel.

That as the voice of Peter in God's church, Pope N. may lead us by example
to set our hearts not on human insight but on divine wisdom.

FOR THE WORLD

That those who set their faces against this world's injustice
may confront worldly powers with the unconquerable witness of truth.

FOR THOSE OPPRESSED, AFFLICTED OR IN NEED

That those who experience society's rejection and persecution
may be vindicated by the God of justice who hears their cry.

That those who face insult because of race or ethnic origin
may stand up for their human dignity.

That the hungry and homeless may find in the hearts of Christians
a faith that manifests itself in practical care and concern for their needs.

FOR THE NEEDS OF THE LOCAL COMMUNITY

That those who work in business and finance
may find courage to bear witness to honesty and integrity above human profit.

That those who are without clothing and lack daily food
may be respected by this community as brothers and sisters in faith.

FOR THE CHRISTIAN ASSEMBLY

That we may find strength in our celebration of the eucharist
to deny ourselves and bear witness in love to Christ and the gospel.

That this community's profession of faith in Jesus the Messiah
may take flesh in practical works of charity for all those in need.

FOR THE DEAD

That the departed whose lives on earth were spent in the service of Christ (especially N.)
may follow Christ now to the salvation promised in the gospel.

Introduction to the Lord's Prayer

As disciples who follow Jesus on the way to the kingdom,
let us pray in childlike trust:

Invitation to Holy Communion

The holy gifts of God for the holy people of God:
Draw near with awe and faith, with praise and thanksgiving.

Dismissal

Seeking to follow the Teacher who came not to be served but to serve,
go in peace to love and serve the Lord.

TWENTY-FIFTH SUNDAY IN ORDINARY TIME
PROPER 20

O God,
whose hand shelters the just and righteous,
and whose favor rests on the lowly,
banish hypocrisy from our hearts
and purify us of all selfish ambition.

Let your word sown among us
bring forth a harvest of peace.

We ask this through our Lord Jesus Christ, your Son,
who lives and reigns with you
in the unity of the Holy Spirit,
God for ever and ever.

By your will, O God, revealed in Christ,
whoever wants to be first must become last of all,
and you have made a little child the measure
    of your kingdom.
Give us the wisdom from above,
that we may welcome the word of your Son
and come to understand that in your sight
the greatest of all is the one who becomes servant
    of all.

We ask this through our Lord Jesus Christ, your Son,
who lives and reigns with you
in the unity of the Holy Spirit,
God for ever and ever.

Roman Lectionary
Wisdom 2:12, 17–20
Psalm 54:3–8
James 3:16 — 4:3
Mark 9:30–37

Revised Common Lectionary
Proverbs 31:10–31
Psalm 1
or
Wisdom of Solomon 1:16 — 2:1, 12–22
or
Jeremiah 11:18–20
Psalm 54
James 3:13 — 4:3, 7–8a
Mark 9:30–37

General Intercessions

Let us pray to God our helper, the Lord, the upholder of our life.

FOR THE CHURCH
That all members of the church may imitate the example of Jesus,
not seeking to be first but becoming servants to all.

FOR THE WORLD
That governments who counter opposition with insult and torture
may not triumph over the righteous or prevail against the just.

That nations may renounce conflicts and disputes,
and realize that a harvest of righteousness is sown in peace for those who make peace.

FOR THOSE OPPRESSED, AFFLICTED OR IN NEED

That those caught up in the quest for power and prestige
may discover that true greatness lies in the humble service of others.

That victims of envy and selfish ambition may not lose faith
but bear witness to the greater power of gentleness and peace.

That all who are persecuted for words or witness
may show by their forbearance the righteousness of their cause.

FOR THE NEEDS OF THE LOCAL COMMUNITY

That those who serve the children of our community in Christ's name
may teach all of us how to welcome Christ in simplicity of heart.

That this parish may be freed from every trace of partiality and hypocrisy
and live by the wisdom from above, full of mercy and good fruits.

FOR THE CHRISTIAN ASSEMBLY

That schooled by the Teacher who became last of all and servant of all
we may go forth from this assembly to serve in gentleness and peace.

That this community may seek in prayer not its own pleasure
but the grace to be of service to others.

FOR THE DEAD

That the dead who were God's children by baptism (especially N.)
may rise again with Jesus to the joy of eternal life.

Introduction to the Lord's Prayer

As disciples who follow Jesus on the way to the kingdom,
let us pray with childlike trust:

Invitation to Holy Communion

The holy gifts of God for the holy people of God:
Draw near with awe and faith, with praise and thanksgiving.

Dismissal

Seeking to follow the Teacher who came not to be served but to serve,
go in peace to love and serve the Lord.

TWENTY-SIXTH SUNDAY IN ORDINARY TIME

PROPER 21

Beyond all human boundaries, O God,
your deeds of power take place,
and your healing mercy is at work.

Ours is not to restrict
the wonders of your saving grace
but to give joyful thanks for your compassion
wherever we may find it.

Teach us to use well the riches of nature and grace
to care generously for those in need
and to look carefully to our own conduct.

We ask this through our Lord Jesus Christ, your Son,
who lives and reigns with you
in the unity of the Holy Spirit,
God for ever and ever.

Never, O God, have you deprived your people
of the voice of your prophets.
Pour forth your Spirit on our assembly and beyond,
as you did in the days of Moses and of Christ's
first disciples.
Adorn every person on the face of the earth with
your gifts,
so that all the peoples of earth may join with us
in proclaiming the mighty wonders your love has
accomplished.

We ask this through our Lord Jesus Christ, your Son,
who lives and reigns with you
in the unity of the Holy Spirit,
God for ever and ever.

Roman Lectionary
Numbers 11:25–29
Psalm 19:8, 10, 12–14
James 5:1–6
Mark 9:38–43, 45, 47–48

Revised Common Lectionary
Esther 7:1–6, 9–10; 9:20–22
Psalm 124
or
Numbers 11:4–6, 10–16, 24–29
Psalm 19:7–14
James 5:13–20
Mark 9:38–50

General Intercessions

To God for whose kingdom we long, let us pray in the name of Christ.

FOR THE CHURCH
That the church may rejoice at every sign of the Spirit's presence
and recognize as fellow disciples all who call on the name of Jesus.

That by sharing decision-making with all God's people,
our leaders may lighten their own burdens and deepen our commitment.

That stumbling blocks placed in the path toward peace
may give way before mutual trust and reconciliation.

FOR THOSE OPPRESSED, AFFLICTED OR IN NEED
That Christians may love and care especially for the little ones of the world,
who bear most clearly the image of the suffering Christ.

That laborers who tend the fields and harvesters who provide for our tables
may receive the just wages and decent living conditions to which they have a right.

FOR THE NEEDS OF THE LOCAL COMMUNITY
That this community may not store up riches for our own profit or pleasure
but generously share with others our material and spiritual treasure.

That Christian landlords and business owners may guard against greed
by opening their hearts to the needy and working on behalf of justice.

FOR THE CHRISTIAN ASSEMBLY
That we who are nourished by the body and blood of Christ
may be wholly dedicated to him in body, mind and spirit.

That we who partake at this table of a foretaste of heaven's banquet
may never choose instead the hell of those who live only for themselves.

FOR THE DEAD
That those who followed Christ in this life and served Christ in others (especially N.)
may come to the reward of life with Christ for ever.

Introduction to the Lord's Prayer

As disciples who follow Jesus on the way to the kingdom,
let us pray in childlike trust:

Invitation to Holy Communion

The holy gifts of God for the holy people of God:
Draw near with awe and faith, with praise and thanksgiving.

Dismissal

Seeking to follow the Teacher who came not to be served but to serve,
go in peace to love and serve the Lord.

TWENTY-SEVENTH SUNDAY IN ORDINARY TIME

PROPER 22

In your image you have made us, O God,
male and female you have made us,
knowing that it is not good for us to be alone.

Penetrate our hard hearts
that we may bind ourselves to one another
fulfilling the splendor of your vision for us.

We ask this through Jesus,
who is not ashamed to call us brothers and sisters,
the high priest who sympathizes with our weakness
and intercedes on our behalf,
Christ Jesus, who is one with you and the Holy Spirit,
God for ever and ever.

O God, you created man and woman
so that the two might share one life,
lived out in freedom and concord,
and reaching toward perfection
under the guidance of your love.
Through the work of your Spirit,
restore to the children of Adam and Eve
the holiness and harmony of creation's earliest days,
and give us faithful hearts,
that what you have joined together
no human power may put asunder.

We ask this through our Lord Jesus Christ, your Son,
who lives and reigns with you
in the unity of the Holy Spirit,
God for ever and ever.

Roman Lectionary
Genesis 2:18 – 24
Psalm 128:1– 6
Hebrews 2:9 –11
Mark 10:2 –12, (13 – 16)

Revised Common Lectionary
Job 1:1; 2:1–10
Psalm 26
or
Genesis 2:18 – 24
Psalm 8
Hebrews 1:1– 4; 2:5 –12
Mark 10:2 –16

General Intercessions

Let us pray to God, for whom and through whom all things exist.

> FOR THE CHURCH
>
> For believers everywhere: May the Lord God deliver us from all hardness of heart
> and make us one in the covenant of fidelity and love.

> FOR THE WORLD
>
> For all peoples of earth: May we celebrate the richness of our diversity and our deeper unity
> as children of the one God and members of the one human family.

For a responsible stewardship of God's good earth and its fragile resources:
May we dwell in harmony with the birds of the air and beasts of the field.

For all who are burdened by loneliness or scarred by rejection:
May they know the joy of loving others and of being loved in return.

For all whose lives are marked by suffering:
May they find hope in Jesus, who was made perfect through suffering.

For those who have experienced the pain of divorce:
May they be supported and sustained by the love of family and friends.

FOR THE NEEDS OF THE LOCAL COMMUNITY

For the married people of our community:
May God help them to persevere as one flesh in one covenant of love.

For those who work in the ministry of marriage preparation:
May God endow them with wise counsel to serve engaged couples.

For those who minister to the children of our parish:
May they reflect to our young the welcoming face of Jesus.

FOR THE CHRISTIAN ASSEMBLY

For this assembly, whom Jesus is not ashamed to call brothers and sisters:
As we sanctify this day to God's glory, may God's grace also sanctify us.

FOR THE DEAD

For those departed ones (especially N.) who put their faith in Jesus:
May they be crowned with glory and honor.

Introduction to the Lord's Prayer

As disciples who follow Jesus on the way to the kingdom,
let us pray with childlike trust:

Invitation to Holy Communion

The holy gifts of God for the holy people of God:
Draw near with awe and faith, with praise and thanksgiving.

Dismissal

Seeking to follow the Teacher who came not to be served but to serve,
go in peace to love and serve the Lord.

TWENTY-EIGHTH SUNDAY IN ORDINARY TIME

PROPER 23

More precious than gold or silver, O God,
more enduring than health and beauty,
is the spirit of your wisdom:
in her hands, uncounted wealth,
in her company, all good gifts!

Send this wisdom from your holy heaven
that we may hear and follow the Good Teacher, Jesus,
who looks on us with love,
and gladly forsake all lesser wealth
for the unrivaled treasure of your kingdom.

We ask this through Jesus,
who is not ashamed to call us brothers and sisters,
the high priest who sympathizes with our weakness
and intercedes on our behalf,
Christ Jesus, who is one with you and the Holy Spirit,
God for ever and ever.

You judge, O God, our thoughts and intentions,
and from your gaze no creature can hide.
Pierce our inmost heart with the two-edged sword of
    your word.
Enlightened by your wisdom,
may we value aright the things of time and of eternity
and, freed from preoccupation with this world's
    wealth,
be poor enough to welcome the incomparable
    treasure of your kingdom.

We ask this through our Lord Jesus Christ, your Son,
who lives and reigns with you
in the unity of the Holy Spirit,
God for ever and ever.

Roman Lectionary
Wisdom 7:7–11
Psalm 90:12–17
Hebrews 4:12–13
Mark 10:17–27, (28–30)

Revised Common Lectionary
Job 23:1–9, 16–17
Psalm 22:1–15
or
Amos 5:6–7, 10–15
Psalm 90:12–17
Hebrews 4:12–16
Mark 10:17–31

General Intercessions

In prayer let us call on God, from whom all good things come.

FOR THE CHURCH
For all who strive to follow Jesus as teacher and Lord:
May we find healing for our divisions and unity of faith in God.

For those who serve God's people in leadership:
May they always prefer God's wisdom to wealth and honor.

For those who guide peoples and nations:
May they govern according to the wisdom that comes from God,
to whom they must one day render an account.

FOR THOSE OPPRESSED, AFFLICTED OR IN NEED

For disciples who endure persecution for the sake of the good news:
May they find courage and strength in Christ's promise of the hundredfold reward.

For those who have worldly wealth and many possessions:
May generous use of their resources liberate them for the kingdom of God.

For those in failing health (especially N.):
May God's wisdom be their unceasing radiance
and the care of family and friends their incomparable wealth.

FOR THE NEEDS OF THE LOCAL COMMUNITY

For those who share God's wisdom with our catechumens and children:
May their teaching enkindle in others an enthusiasm for discipleship.

For our parish:
May God's word refine the thoughts and intentions of every heart.

FOR THE CHRISTIAN ASSEMBLY

For this assembly's growth in discipleship:
May we leave behind whatever hinders our following of Christ.

FOR THE DEAD

For those who lived the good news in this life (especially N.):
May they receive eternal life in the age to come.

Introduction to the Lord's Prayer

As disciples who follow Jesus on the way to the kingdom,
let us pray with childlike trust:

Invitation to Holy Communion

The holy gifts of God for the holy people of God:
Draw near with awe and faith, with praise and thanksgiving.

Dismissal

Seeking to follow the Teacher who came not to be served but to serve,
go in peace to love and serve the Lord.

TWENTY-NINTH SUNDAY IN ORDINARY TIME

PROPER 24

Maker and author of life,
in Jesus we have found the path to wisdom.

Let us, therefore, be bold to approach you,
not seeking privilege but asking mercy.
Let us live among one another,
not seeking to be served but to serve.

We ask this through Jesus,
who is not ashamed to call us brothers and sisters,
the high priest who sympathizes with our weakness
and intercedes on our behalf,
Christ Jesus, who is one with you and the Holy Spirit,
God for ever and ever.

God of pardon and peace,
in Christ you have given us a great high priest
who has entered the sanctuary of heaven
to intercede for us in the power of the sacrifice
offered once, for all, to take away our sin.
Grant that all of us may receive your mercy
and find grace to help in our time of need.
May we drink fully from the chalice of Christ's
own suffering
that we may come to share in the eternal life
won by the redeeming death of Jesus,
who lives and reigns with you
in the unity of the Holy Spirit,
God for ever and ever.

Roman Lectionary
Isaiah 53:10–11
Psalm 33:4–5, 18–19, 20, 22
Hebrews 4:14–16
Mark 10:(35–41), 42–45

Revised Common Lectionary
Job 38:1–7, (34–41)
Psalm 104: 1–9, 24, 35c
or
Isaiah 53:4–12
Psalm 91:9–16
Hebrews 5:1–10
Mark 10:35–45

General Intercessions

Let us approach the throne of grace with confidence,
praying in the name of Jesus, our great high priest.

FOR THE CHURCH
That all God's people, especially those in positions of authority, may imitate the example of Jesus,
who came not to be served but to serve.

That God may protect the church from the lure of power and prestige,
that we may bear witness in the world to Jesus' self-sacrificing love.

FOR THE WORLD

That politicians and elected officials may recall the source of their power
and seek their greatness only by making themselves the servants of all.

FOR THOSE OPPRESSED, AFFLICTED OR IN NEED

That all who struggle for justice under the rule of tyrants
may sustain their cause in righteousness and achieve their liberation.

That those who are crushed by anguish of heart or emotional pain
may come to the light of God's peace and a knowledge of God's purpose.

That those afflicted by the infirmity of age or the burden of disease
may derive strength from their union with Christ, the Servant of the Lord.

FOR THE NEEDS OF THE LOCAL COMMUNITY

That we may gladly dedicate our community's time and resources
to the relief of those abandoned by society.

That those who are discouraged by personal weakness
may find in our community the sympathy and support of fellow pilgrims.

That our catechumens may persevere
in their preparation for baptism into Christ's death and resurrection.

FOR THE CHRISTIAN ASSEMBLY

That this assembly, nourished at the sacrifice of the Lord's own Servant,
may gladly bear the burdens of others and seek to serve in sacrificial love.

FOR THE DEAD

That all the dead who held fast to their confession of faith on earth (especially N.)
may pass through the heavens to stand with joy before the throne of grace.

Introduction to the Lord's Prayer

As disciples who follow Jesus on the way to the kingdom,
let us pray with childlike trust:

Invitation to Holy Communion

The holy gifts of God for the holy people of God:
Draw near with awe and faith, with praise and thanksgiving.

Dismissal

Seeking to follow the Teacher who came not to be served but to serve,
go in peace to love and serve the Lord.

THIRTIETH SUNDAY IN ORDINARY TIME

PROPER 25

God our Savior,
from the ends of the earth
you gather the weak and the lowly.
You make them a great and glad multitude,
refreshed and renewed at your hand.
Throwing off the burden of sin,
they run to the Teacher for healing.

Let the faith Christ bestows
restore to the church this vision
of the gathering that embraces the weary and
    wounded of this world.

We ask this through the Christ
who was, who is and who is to come,
your Son who lives and reigns with you
in the unity of the Holy Spirit,
God for ever and ever.

O God, light to the blind and joy to the afflicted,
in your only-begotten Son you have given us
    a high priest
who is just and compassionate
toward those who groan beneath the burden of
    oppression and sorrow.
Listen, then, to the cry of our prayer:
May all who are in need recognize you in Jesus
    of Nazareth
and gladly follow Jesus on the way that leads to you.

We ask this through our Lord Jesus Christ, your Son,
who lives and reigns with you
in the unity of the Holy Spirit,
God for ever and ever.

Roman Lectionary	**Revised Common Lectionary**
Jeremiah 31:7–9	Job 42:1–6, 10–17
Psalm 126:1–6	Psalm 34:1–8, (19–22)
Hebrews 5:1–6	*or*
Mark 10:46–52	Jeremiah 31:7–9
	Psalm 126
	Hebrews 7:23–28
	Mark 10:46–52

General Intercessions

Through Jesus, the Son of David, let us pray in faith for all God's people.

FOR THE CHURCH
That God may gather from the farthest parts of the earth
a faithful remnant to proclaim and give praise to God's name.

That those in the ordained ministry may reflect the gentleness of Christ
and serve the wayward in the humble awareness of their own weaknesses.

FOR THE WORLD

That nations may not stumble on the path that leads to peace
but walk to that goal by the straight path of justice and mutual respect.

FOR THOSE OPPRESSED, AFFLICTED OR IN NEED

That society may provide special care for the poor who are most in need:
those who are blind or lame, those with child and those who care for their children or grandchildren.

That Christians may never neglect or silence those who cry out for help
but gladly share with them the resources the Lord has given us.

FOR THE NEEDS OF THE LOCAL COMMUNITY

That our catechumens may receive the gift of spiritual insight,
which will join them to our community in following Jesus on the way.

That those who are bereaved may pass through their time of weeping
and receive the consolations of this community's care and support.

That the sick of our community (especially N.) may receive the healing born of faith.

FOR THE CHRISTIAN ASSEMBLY

That we who are baptized as a priestly people may offer fitting worship here and in the world,
the living and acceptable sacrifice of charity to all.

That our eucharistic assembly may faithfully call out to Jesus for mercy
and lovingly extend to others the mercy so freely bestowed on us.

FOR THE DEAD

That our faithful departed (especially N.) may be gathered to that great company
whom God will lead to the waters of eternal life.

Introduction to the Lord's Prayer

As disciples who follow Jesus on the way to the kingdom,
let us pray with childlike trust:

Invitation to Holy Communion

The holy gifts of God for the holy people of God:
Draw near with awe and faith, with praise and thanksgiving.

Dismissal

Seeking to follow the Teacher who came not to be served but to serve,
go in peace to love and serve the Lord.

THIRTY-FIRST SUNDAY IN ORDINARY TIME

PROPER 26

You are one God, O Lord,
and beside you there is no other.
You alone are we to love
with all our heart,
with all our soul,
with all our strength,
and our neighbor as ourselves.

Sharpen our ears
to hear this great commandment.
Arouse our hearts
to offer this twofold love.

We ask this through the Christ who was,
who is and who is to come:
your Son who lives and reigns with you
in the unity of the Holy Spirit,
God for ever and ever.

You alone, O Lord our God, are the one true God,
and there is no other God besides you.
Grant us the grace to listen,
that our hearts, our minds and our senses
may be open to receive the word that saves,
the gospel of Jesus, our eternal high priest,
who lives and reigns with you
in the unity of the Holy Spirit,
God for ever and ever.

Roman Lectionary
Deuteronomy 6:2 – 6
Psalm 18:2 – 5, 47, 51
Hebrews 7:23 – 28
Mark 12:28 – 34

Revised Common Lectionary
Ruth 1:1–18
Psalm 146
or
Deuteronomy 6:1– 9
Psalm 119:1– 8
Hebrews 9:11–14
Mark 12:28 – 34

General Intercessions

To the Lord our God, let us pray through Jesus our high priest,
who forever lives to make intercession for us.

FOR THE CHURCH
For all who reverence the Lord, the God of our ancestors:
May we diligently keep the commandments and grow in mutual respect.

For the gift of peace for our children and our children's children:
May a love based on justice multiply greatly in this and in every land.

For an end to all disputes based on religious issues and observances:
May believers see that love is more important than offerings and sacrifices.

FOR THOSE OPPRESSED, AFFLICTED OR IN NEED

For those displaced from ancestral lands by violence and discord:
May society grow in respect for the unique cultural heritage of others.

For the healing of those in spiritual or emotional distress:
May compassion embrace them through those who minister in Jesus' name.

FOR THE NEEDS OF THE LOCAL COMMUNITY

For the catechumens as they look to believers for guidance and inspiration:
May this community teach the commandments by putting them into practice.

For our parish's ministries of social justice and community service:
May this work give flesh and blood to the command to love our neighbor.

FOR THE CHRISTIAN ASSEMBLY

For the right ordering of our priorities:
May love of God and neighbor be the measure and meaning of our lives.

FOR THE DEAD

For all the dead whose lives bore witness to Jesus' commandment of love (especially N.):
May they enter into the land of promise that flows with the milk and honey of eternal life.

Introduction to the Lord's Prayer

Let us pray in the words of the One whose coming is certain
and whose day draws near:

Invitation to Holy Communion

They will come from east and west and from north and south to sit at the table in the kingdom of God:
Blessed are those who are called to the banquet of the Lamb.

Dismissal

In the name of Jesus Christ the faithful witness, who is, who was and who is to come,
go in peace to love and serve the Lord.

THIRTY-SECOND SUNDAY IN ORDINARY TIME

PROPER 27

Robed in glory before all time, O God,
your Son was stripped and mocked.
Enthroned in glory at your side,
Christ was lifted up on the cross.
Equal to you in the splendor of divinity,
Jesus emptied himself for our salvation.

Fix our eyes on this self-surrender,
stir up our hearts to give freely and generously
all that we are and all that we have
for the coming of your kingdom.

We ask this through the Christ
who was, who is and who is to come:
your Son who lives and reigns with you
in the unity of the Holy Spirit,
God for ever and ever.

O God, protector of the widow and orphan,
safe haven for strangers,
justice for the oppressed,
uphold the poor who hope in you
and sustain those who place their trust in your love.
Let no one be deprived
of the bread and freedom you provide,
but may all people learn to share freely and generously
of the good gifts you have bestowed,
following the example of Jesus,
who offered his very life for our salvation,
and who lives and reigns with you
in the unity of the Holy Spirit,
God for ever and ever.

Roman Lectionary	**Revised Common Lectionary**
1 Kings 17:10–16	Ruth 3:1–5; 4:13–17
Psalm 146:7–10	Psalm 127
Hebrews 9:24–28	*or*
Mark 12:38–44	1 Kings 17:8–16
	Psalm 146
	Hebrews 9:24–28
	Mark 12:38–44

General Intercessions

Let us pray for the needs of all to God our provider,
through Jesus who intercedes in the presence of God on our behalf.

FOR THE CHURCH

That the church may generously share its material and spiritual resources,
trusting in the Lord God to provide for all its needs.

That the church's leaders may renounce every desire for power and prestige,
serving God's people in humility after the example of the Master.

That nations may cooperate in the effective distribution of earth's produce,
seeking to provide especially for those in most need.

FOR THOSE OPPRESSED, AFFLICTED OR IN NEED

That those who suffer from drought and famine may find relief,
receiving rain from the heavens and food from the earth.

That those burdened by sin and guilt may be delivered to know true peace,
seeing in Jesus the priest who offered himself to bear the sins of all.

FOR THE NEEDS OF THE LOCAL COMMUNITY

That our community may imitate the sacrificial love of Jesus,
giving not only out of our abundance but out of our life's very sustenance.

That the catechumens of the church may find new life in the gospel,
meeting in Christ the One who saves those who are eagerly waiting for him.

FOR THE CHRISTIAN ASSEMBLY

That we may beware of making an empty show of our religious practice,
striving instead to let our faith transform us into true servants of the gospel.

That we may be transformed by the bounty we receive in this eucharist,
learning to feed the hungry as the Lord has graciously fed us.

FOR THE DEAD

That those who have died (especially N.) may experience a merciful judgment,
receiving the salvation won for them by Christ's sacrifice.

Introduction to the Lord's Prayer

In the name of Jesus, whose words are guiding creation to fulfillment,
let us pray for the coming of the kingdom:

Invitation to Holy Communion

They will come from east and west and from north and south to sit at the table in the kingdom of God:
Blessed are those who are called to the banquet of the Lamb.

Dismissal

In the name of Jesus Christ the faithful witness, who is, who was and who is to come,
go in peace to love and serve the Lord.

THIRTY-THIRD SUNDAY IN ORDINARY TIME

PROPER 28

In every generation, O God,
your purpose presses on toward fulfillment.
Near indeed is the One whose words will not
 pass away.

Ready us to face whatever anguish attends
the accomplishment of your will for creation.
As you gather your elect from the ends of the earth,
count us also among those
whose names are written in the book of life.

We ask this through the Christ
who was, who is and who is to come:
your Son who lives and reigns with you
in the unity of the Holy Spirit,
God for ever and ever.

You keep vigil, O God,
over the fortunes of your people,
guiding their destiny in safety
as the history of the world unfolds.
Increase our faith
that those who sleep in the dust of the earth
 shall rise again,
and give us your Spirit
to bring forth in our lives the fruit of charity,
so that we may look forward every day
to the glorious manifestation of your Son,
who will come to gather the elect in your kingdom.

We ask this through our Lord Jesus Christ, your Son,
who lives and reigns with you
in the unity of the Holy Spirit,
God for ever and ever.

Roman Lectionary	**Revised Common Lectionary**
Daniel 12:1–3	1 Samuel 1:4–20
Psalm 16:5, 8–11	1 Samuel 2:1–10
Hebrews 10:11–14, 18	*or*
Mark 13:24–32	Daniel 12:1–3
	Psalm 16
	Hebrews 10:11–14, (15–18), 19–25
	Mark 13:1–8

General Intercessions

As creation moves toward fulfillment, let us pray through the Son of Man,
who is coming with great power and glory.

FOR THE CHURCH
That the church may faithfully share the wisdom handed on to it by God
and lead many to righteousness as the day of the Lord draws near.

That God's people may be delivered in times of anguish
and so be able to protect and serve those who have no one to help them.

That nations and peoples engulfed in conflict may find the path to peace
and not inherit the shame and contempt of having forfeited the gift of life.

FOR THOSE OPPRESSED, AFFLICTED OR IN NEED

That those in any anguish of body, mind or spirit may find hope in Christ's words
and help from Christ's disciples.

That those who suffer hunger may receive the food they need
from the just sharing of the bounty of earth's harvests.

That innocent victims of lawless deeds may find peace in the love of Christ
and in the care of those devoted to their healing.

FOR THE NEEDS OF THE LOCAL COMMUNITY

That our community may serve as an angel of healing and protection
to those in this area who suffer from homelessness or hunger.

That the sick of our community (especially N.) may deepen their sanctification
as they unite their sufferings to the perfect offering of Christ.

FOR THE CHRISTIAN ASSEMBLY

That our communion in prayer with God's elect throughout the earth
may deepen our sense of partnership in the church's worldwide mission.

That our eucharistic worship may stir us to bear witness to gospel justice
as we proclaim that even now Christ is near, at the very gates.

FOR THE DEAD

That our beloved departed whose bodies sleep in the dust of the earth (especially N.)
may awake to everlasting life and shine like the stars for all eternity.

Introduction to the Lord's Prayer

In the name of Jesus, whose words are guiding creation to fulfillment,
let us pray for the coming of the kingdom:

Invitation to Holy Communion

They will come from east and west and from north and south to sit at the table in the kingdom of God:
Blessed are those who are called to the banquet of the Lamb.

Dismissal

In the name of Jesus Christ the faithful witness, who is, who was and who is to come,
go in peace to love and serve the Lord.

THIRTY-FOURTH SUNDAY IN ORDINARY TIME

CHRIST THE KING
PROPER 29

Lord God almighty,
you have anointed Jesus as the Christ
not to rule a kingdom won by violence
but to bear witness to the truth,
not to reign in arrogance
but to serve in humility and love,
not to mirror this world's powers
but to inherit a dominion that will not pass away.

Freed from our sins
by the blood of this faithful witness,
shape our service of others
after the pattern of Christ's self-sacrificing love.

We ask this through the Christ
who was, who is and who is to come,
your Son who lives and reigns with you
in the unity of the Holy Spirit,
God for ever and ever.

Eternal God, whose days are from before time
    and for endless ages,
you sent your Son in the fullness of time
to make us a kingdom of priests in your service.
Teach us that to serve is to reign,
that by giving our lives over completely
to the service of our brothers and sisters,
we may offer an authentic profession
of our loyalty to Jesus Christ,
the faithful witness, the firstborn of the dead
and the ruler of the kings of the earth,
who lives and reigns with you
in the unity of the Holy Spirit,
God for ever and ever.

Roman Lectionary
Daniel 7:13–14
Psalm 93:1–2, 5
Revelation 1:5–8
John 18:33b–37

Revised Common Lectionary
2 Samuel 23:1–7
Psalm 132:1–12, (13–18)
or
Daniel 7:9–10, 13–14
Psalm 93
Revelation 1:4b–8
John 18:33–37

General Intercessions

Let us pray to God in the name of Jesus, the ruler of the kings of earth,
whose dominion is everlasting and whose kingship shall never be destroyed.

FOR THE CHURCH
That Christians may imitate Jesus their king
by renouncing worldly power and bearing witness to Christ's kingdom of justice, love and peace.

That those who govern nations and guide the destinies of peoples
may listen to the voice of Truth and seek the paths of peace and justice.

FOR THOSE OPPRESSED, AFFLICTED OR IN NEED
For all who reflect the image of Christ the King in the humiliation of the passion:
May all the tribes of earth learn to lament our inhumanity to one another.

That all whose hearts are pierced by sorrow or whose dignity is wounded
may find help in time of need and hope in the ultimate triumph of Truth.

FOR THE NEEDS OF THE LOCAL COMMUNITY
For catechumens preparing to declare their allegiance to Christ's reign:
May they find in this community the living witness of Christ's followers.

For those who are unemployed or handicapped, hungry or homeless:
May our community's response herald the dawning of Christ's kingdom.

That all who are seeking God or striving to know the truth
may find in the life of our community the faith and love that point to Christ.

That those who feel powerless in the face of life's difficulties
may find helping hands and loving hearts in our community.

FOR THE CHRISTIAN ASSEMBLY
For this assembly, fashioned by Christ into a kingdom of priests:
May our worship glorify God and our witness announce Christ's reign.

FOR THE DEAD
That those who in this life looked for the coming of Christ's kingdom (especially N.)
may find in eternal life the fullness of Christ's glorious reign.

Introduction to the Lord's Prayer

Let us pray in the words of the One whose coming is certain
and whose day draws near:

Invitation to Holy Communion

They will come from east and west and from north and south to sit at the table in the kingdom of God:
Blessed are those who are called to the banquet of the Lamb.

Dismissal

In the name of Jesus Christ the faithful witness, who is, who was and who is to come,
go in peace to love and serve the Lord.

HOLY TRINITY
SUNDAY AFTER PENTECOST

Lord our God,
whose voice we have heard in our midst,
whose face we have seen in Christ Jesus,
and whose Spirit dwells within us:

Baptized in your name,
we embrace what Jesus has commanded us.
Remembering that Jesus is with us always,
we pray that our worship be acceptable
and our witness effective,
in the power of the Spirit
who makes us your children.

We ask this through our Lord Jesus Christ, your Son,
who lives and reigns with you
in the unity of the Holy Spirit,
God for ever and ever.

O God Most High,
in the waters of baptism
you made us your sons and daughters
in Christ, your only-begotten Son.
Hear deep within us the cry of that Spirit,
who calls out to you, "Abba, Father,"
and grant that, obedient to our Savior's commission,
we may become heralds of the salvation you offer
    to all
and go forth to make disciples of all nations.

We ask this through our Lord Jesus Christ, your Son,
who lives and reigns with you
in the unity of the Holy Spirit,
God for ever and ever.

Roman Lectionary	**Revised Common Lectionary**
Deuteronomy 4:32–34, 39–40	Isaiah 6:1–8
Psalm 33:4–6, 9, 18–20, 22	Psalm 29
Romans 8:14–17	Romans 8:12–17
Matthew 28:16–20	John 3:1–17

General Intercessions

Let us pray without fear as a people loved by the Lord,
who has done mighty deeds for us.

FOR THE CHURCH
For the church, sent to make disciples of all nations:
May we teach what Christ has commanded in the gospel of love.

FOR THE WORLD
For all the peoples of earth, created in God's image:
May the world find the way to peace in God's statutes and commandments.

For those enslaved by human oppression or inner fears:
May the Spirit within them lead them to the freedom of the children of God.

FOR THE NEEDS OF THE LOCAL COMMUNITY

For married couples, for parents and children, for those who live in religious or service communities:
May their mutual love reflect to all the image of the Triune God.

For the sick and suffering members of our community (especially N.):
May they find strength in joining their sufferings to those of Christ
and hope in the assurance of being glorified with Christ.

FOR THE CHRISTIAN ASSEMBLY

For all of us:
May our love and service of others bear witness to the nearness of God's abiding love.

FOR THE DEAD

For those disciples who have died in Christ (especially N.):
Heirs of God, may they live forever in the land God has destined for us.

Introduction to the Lord's Prayer

Because in Christ we have received the Spirit of adoption,
as sons and daughters of God we dare to pray:

Invitation to Holy Communion

The holy gifts of God for the holy people of God:
Draw near with awe and faith, with praise and thanksgiving.

Dismissal

Children of God, joint heirs with Christ and led by the Spirit,
go in peace to love and serve the Lord.

THE BODY AND BLOOD OF CHRIST
SUNDAY AFTER HOLY TRINITY

Faithful God,
whose everlasting covenant with us
is sealed in the blood of Christ,
be present in our midst,
in the assembly of your people:
For all that you command us we will do.

In the book of the covenant, speak to our hearts.
By the blood of the covenant, purify our consciences.
As we give thanks with bread and cup
for the mercy that has found us,
gather all your children in forgiveness.

We ask this through the mediator
who pleads on our behalf, Jesus Christ,
who lives and reigns with you
in the unity of the Holy Spirit,
God for ever and ever.

Behold, O God,
your people gathered here around this altar
to offer you the sacrifice of the new and
    everlasting covenant.
Purify our consciences to worship you, the living God,
so that at this supper of the Lamb,
we may delight in a foretaste of the eternal Pasch,
which your saints celebrate forever
    in the heavenly Jerusalem.

We ask this through our Lord Jesus Christ, your Son,
who lives and reigns with you
in the unity of the Holy Spirit,
God for ever and ever.

Roman Lectionary
Exodus 24:3 – 8
Psalm 147:12 –15, 19 – 20
Hebrews 9:11–15
Mark 14:12 –16, 22 – 26

General Intercessions

As we worship the living God, let us lift up our voices in prayer
through Christ, the high priest and mediator of the new covenant.

FOR THE CHURCH
That all the people of God, treasuring the book of the covenant,
may live in peace by obeying the Lord's words and ordinances.

FOR THE WORLD
That all the peoples of earth, redeemed by the blood of the covenant,
may reverence each other as children of the one God who has chosen them.

That those who have defiled themselves by espousing prejudice or racism
may allow the blood of Christ to purify their consciences and hearts.

FOR THE NEEDS OF THE LOCAL COMMUNITY
That those who prepare our young people to share in the eucharist
and those who bring communion to our sick and homebound
may be living signs of the presence of Christ, who is our Passover and our Peace.

FOR THE CHRISTIAN ASSEMBLY
That we who are graced in this eucharist with the book of the covenant, the broken bread
and the cup of blessing
may offer our lives as a living sacrifice of praise to God and service to all.

FOR THE DEAD
That by the death of Christ that redeems them, the faithful departed (especially N.)
may receive the promised eternal inheritance.

Introduction to the Lord's Prayer

With trust in God whose providence nourishes and sustains us,
we pray now as Jesus taught us.

Invitation to Holy Communion

Behold the living bread come down from heaven: Those who eat of it will never die.
This is the cup of eternal life: Those who drink of it will live for ever.

Dismissal

Nourished at the Lord's table and obedient to God's covenant,
go in peace to love and serve the Lord.

THE SACRED HEART OF JESUS
FRIDAY FOLLOWING SECOND SUNDAY AFTER PENTECOST

With tender compassion, O God, and not with wrath,
you have come into our midst
and lifted us to your heart,
binding us with love.

Center our hearts in this love
and keep it ever before our eyes.
As we look on the One whom we have pierced,
remind us that we are cleansed in that blood
    and water.
As we bear witness to your love in the world,
reveal to us in those we serve
brothers and sisters dear to your heart.

We ask this through Christ,
who dwells in our hearts by faith,
and who lives and reigns with you
in the unity of the Holy Spirit,
God for ever and ever.

O God, whose bounty is infinite
and whose tender compassion never fails,
with tireless care you sustain your sons and daughters
and open wide your hand to provide for their
    nourishment.
Fix our eyes on the heart of your Christ,
pierced for us on the cross,
and help us to recognize there
the sublime and boundless riches of your love.
Renewed by the power of your Spirit,
may we proclaim to others
the love of Christ that surpasses knowledge
and gladly share with them the treasure
    of redemption.

We ask this through our Lord Jesus Christ, your Son,
who lives and reigns with you
in the unity of the Holy Spirit,
God for ever and ever.

Roman Lectionary
Hosea 11:1, 3 – 4, 8c – 9
Isaiah 12:2 – 6
Ephesians 3:8 – 12, 14 – 19
John 19:31 – 37

General Intercessions

With confidence born of faith,
let us pray in the name of Christ Jesus our Lord.

FOR THE CHURCH
For the church throughout the world:
May it make known to all people the wisdom of God.

FOR THE WORLD
For the nations of the earth:
May God draw the world to unity and peace with cords of human kindness.

FOR THOSE OPPRESSED, AFFLICTED OR IN NEED
For the brokenhearted:
May God's healing love come to them through the compassion of believers.

FOR THE NEEDS OF THE LOCAL COMMUNITY
For the families of this community:
May they be grounded in love and strengthened by God's Spirit.

For those preparing to enter marriage or the ministry:
May they know and share the love of Christ.

FOR THE CHRISTIAN ASSEMBLY
For this community of faith,
cleansed in the blood and water flowing from the heart of Christ:
May we believe and bear witness to the love by which we are redeemed.

For this eucharistic assembly:
May Christ dwell in our hearts by faith and shine in the witness of our lives.

FOR THE DEAD
For those who have died (especially N.):
May they come to know with all the saints the breadth and length and height and depth
    of Christ's love.

Introduction to the Lord's Prayer

Because in Christ we have received the Spirit of adoption,
as sons and daughters of God we dare to pray:

Invitation to Holy Communion

The holy gifts of God for the holy people of God:
Draw near with awe and faith, with praise and thanksgiving.

Dismissal

Entrusted with the good news of the boundless love of the heart of Christ,
go in peace to love and serve the Lord.

2
FEBRUARY
THE PRESENTATION OF THE LORD

God of light,
your Son shared our flesh and blood
and built us into a living temple
where you might dwell.

Like Simeon and Anna,
our eyes behold your salvation.
Guide us by the Spirit to welcome your Christ
as the Gentiles' light and Israel's glory
by whose sacrifice we are presented before you
to be the people of your covenant.

We ask this through our Lord Jesus Christ,
Emmanuel, God with us,
your Son who lives and reigns with you
in the unity of the Holy Spirit,
God for ever and ever.

In the midst of your temple, O God,
we ponder your loving kindness.
In the darkness of the shadow of death,
we greet the messenger of light and life.
We look on the face of a helpless infant
and see the divine countenance
before whom the angels of heaven veil their faces.

Today we have lighted the candles we bear
from the Light of the World
whom Simeon carries in his arms.
May the light of faith that illumines our hearts
shine brightly before the throne of your mercy,
and may the fire of charity enkindled in our lives
bring warmth and joy to our brothers and sisters.

We ask this through our Lord Jesus Christ, your Son,
who lives and reigns with you
in the unity of the Holy Spirit,
God for ever and ever.

Roman Lectionary
Malachi 3:1–4
Psalm 24:7–10
Hebrews 2:14–18
Luke 2:22–40

Revised Common Lectionary
Malachi 3:1–4
Psalm 84 *or* Psalm 24:7–10
Hebrews 2:14–18
Luke 2:22–40

General Intercessions

Let us present our prayer through Jesus, the true Light of the World,
the merciful high priest, who is not ashamed to call us brothers and sisters.

FOR THE CHURCH
For the church commissioned to preach Christ's gospel,
that its bold and faithful witness may make it a light of revelation, a sign of contradiction
and a haven of consolation.

For peoples enslaved by violence and terrorism,
that respect and understanding may destroy the power of hatred and death.

For those whose faith is tested by life's burdens and pain,
that Jesus, who himself was tested by suffering, may be their strength.

For the parents and children of this parish,
that they may grow stronger in love and be filled with God's wisdom.

For the senior citizens of our community,
that their insightful wisdom and devout prayer may inspire and guide younger parishioners.

For all of us gathered in this holy temple,
that, refined by God's word and purified by the Lord's sacrifice,
we may bear the light of Christ to others.

For those who looked forward in this life to the redemption won by Christ (especially N.),
that, freed from the power of death, they may rejoice in eternal light.

Introduction to the Lord's Prayer

Because in Christ we have received the Spirit of adoption,
as sons and daughters of God we dare to pray:

Invitation to Holy Communion

Behold the true Light of the World, the Beloved of God, anointed by the Spirit.
Blessed are those who are called to the banquet of the Lamb.

Dismissal

Enlightened by Christ and anointed by the Spirit,
go now in peace to love and serve the Lord.

24
JUNE
THE BIRTH OF JOHN THE BAPTIST

God of the covenant,
whose promises can never fail,
in every age you place your words
on the lips of the prophets
and a thirst for justice in the hearts of your people.

As we celebrate the birth of John the Baptist,
preacher of your word and herald of the Savior,
challenge us with the conversion John proclaimed
and comfort us with the salvation he announced.

We ask this through our Lord Jesus Christ,
who was, who is and who is to come,
your Son, who lives and reigns with you
in the unity of the Holy Spirit,
God for ever and ever.

From his mother's womb, O God of Israel,
you called John the Baptist to be your Son's herald,
and in the solitude of the desert
you fashioned him into your polished arrow,
placing your words in his mouth,
to uproot and to pull down,
to destroy and to overthrow,
to build and to plant.

As John's preaching shook the world
from its indifference
and prepared your people for the advent of the Christ,
so let our celebration of his birth
confront our complacency with the call to conversion
and prepare us for the day of Christ's glorious return.

We ask this through our Lord Jesus Christ, your Son,
who lives and reigns with you
in the unity of the Holy Spirit,
God for ever and ever.

Roman Lectionary

VIGIL	DAY
Jeremiah 1:4–10	Isaiah 49:1–6
Psalm 71:1–6, 15, 17	Psalm 71:1–6, 15, 17
1 Peter 1:8–12	Acts 13:22–26
Luke 1:5–17	Luke 1:57–66, 80

General Intercessions

Let us offer our prayers to the Lord our God,
who called John the Baptist to be prophet and herald,
and who has given us new birth to living hope by Christ's resurrection.

FOR THE CHURCH

That the church may be a light to the nations,
speaking what God commands and announcing the Christ
who is coming with judgment and salvation.

FOR THE WORLD

That the word of God may resound over nations and over kingdoms,
pulling down injustice, planting truth and building righteousness.

FOR THE OPPRESSED

That God may restore courage to those who feel they have labored in vain
and renew the commitment of those whose strength is spent.

FOR THE NEEDS OF THE LOCAL COMMUNITY

That the children of our community may grow and become strong in spirit
as they discern the Lord's call to embrace their future.

That the seniors of our community, like Zechariah and Elizabeth,
may witness to us by persevering prayer and trust in God's providence.

FOR THE CHRISTIAN ASSEMBLY

That although we have not seen the Messiah heralded by John the Baptist,
we may believe and rejoice in receiving the outcome of faith, our salvation.

FOR THE DEAD

That those who have died in Christ (especially N.)
may receive the salvation announced by John and bestowed by Christ.

Introduction to the Lord's Prayer

Because in Christ we have received the Spirit of adoption,
as sons and daughters of God we dare to pray:

Invitation to Holy Communion

Behold the Lamb of God, who takes away the sin of the world.
Blessed are those who are called to the banquet of the Lamb.

Dismissal

As heralds of the Messiah proclaimed by John the Baptist,
go in peace to love and serve the Lord.

29
JUNE
PETER AND PAUL, APOSTLES

Your grace, O God of new life,
transformed Peter's denials of the Lord
and Paul's persecution of the church
into a mighty witness of bold preaching,
faithful serving and sacrificial love
even unto death.

On us who give thanks this day
for the inheritance of these apostles,
bestow your grace in abundant measure
that we, with them, may fight the good fight,
finish the race, keep the faith
and receive at last the crown of righteousness.

We ask this through our Lord Jesus Christ, your Son,
who lives and reigns with you
in the unity of the Holy Spirit,
God for ever and ever.

God of all nations,
your saving plan embraces Jews and Gentiles,
and you long to gather into one communion
all your children now scattered over the face
    of the earth.

As we praise your grace in the apostles Peter and Paul,
confirm us in the heritage they handed on to us.
Make your church stand firm on the rock of faith,
even as the love of Christ impels us forward in the
    freedom of the Spirit.
May the rich diversity of gifts and insights
that adorn your church in every age
strengthen the effectiveness of its witness
and bind us together in the unity of faith and love.

We ask this through our Lord Jesus Christ, your Son,
who lives and reigns with you
in the unity of the Holy Spirit,
God for ever and ever.

Roman Lectionary

VIGIL	DAY
Acts 3:1–10	Acts 12:1–11
Psalm 19:2 – 5	Psalm 34:2 – 9
Galatians 1:11– 20	2 Timothy 4:6 – 8, 17–18
John 21:15 –19	Matthew 16:13 –19

General Intercessions

On this solemnity of Saints Peter and Paul,
let the church pray fervently to God in the name of Jesus of Nazareth.

FOR THE CHURCH
That the church, built on Peter's faith and formed by the preaching of Paul,
may be a light to the nations and the sacrament of their salvation.

That the hostile powers of earth may not prevail against the gospel
and all the nations that long for truth may hear the message fully proclaimed.

FOR THOSE OPPRESSED, AFFLICTED OR IN NEED

That those who lay violent hands on God's servants may be converted,
and those imprisoned for conscience's sake may persevere in their witness.

That Pope N., bishop of that church whose beginnings were consecrated by the witness
    of Peter and Paul,
may lead us in professing our faith and inspire us in preaching the gospel.

That those who have been sent to proclaim Christ among the nations
may experience the Lord standing by them to give them strength.

FOR THE NEEDS OF THE LOCAL COMMUNITY

That those who pour out their lives in service to the destitute
may keep faith with the gospel and persevere in their witness.

That the sick and suffering of this community (especially N.)
may find health and healing in the name of Jesus of Nazareth.

FOR THE CHRISTIAN ASSEMBLY

That we who are the descendants in faith of Saints Peter and Paul
may gladly share the salvation that is ours in the name of Jesus of Nazareth.

FOR THE DEAD

That all who in life longed for the Lord's appearing (especially N.)
may receive from the Lord the crown of righteousness.

Introduction to the Lord's Prayer

Because in Christ we have received the Spirit of adoption,
as sons and daughters of God we dare to pray:

Invitation to Holy Communion

The holy gifts of God for the holy people of God:
Draw near with awe and faith, with praise and thanksgiving.

Dismissal

Giving thanks to God who has called us to share the inheritance of the saints in light,
go in peace to love and serve the Lord.

6
AUGUST
THE TRANSFIGURATION OF THE LORD

O God, whose Son, your Beloved,
was transfigured in dazzling light,
with reverent awe we enter your holy presence.

Your presence cannot be contained
in tents our hands have made
but must be sought in your creatures
and all that your hands have fashioned.
Lead us from the high mountain
to seek you in the lowly of the earth,
serving them, after Christ's example,
in peace and sacrificial love.

We ask this through our Lord Jesus Christ, your Son,
who lives and reigns with you
in the unity of the Holy Spirit,
God for ever and ever.

God of life,
in a blaze of light on Mount Tabor
you transfigured Christ,
revealing him as your Beloved Son
and promising us a share in that destiny of glory.

But in a blinding flash of weaponry,
we, children of that promise, annihilated life,
disfiguring the face of Christ
and mocking his gospel call to gentleness and peace.

Let the beacon of that gospel
pierce again the clouds enshrouding the earth,
so that even in the darkness of these times
we may believe your day will dawn.

We ask this through our Lord Jesus Christ, your Son,
who lives and reigns with you
in the unity of the Holy Spirit,
God for ever and ever.

Roman Lectionary
Daniel 7:9–10, 13–14
Psalm 97:1–2, 5–6, 9
2 Peter 1:16–19
Mark 9:2–10

Revised Common Lectionary
In many churches, the Transfiguration is commemorated on the Sunday before Ash Wednesday. The readings for that day are:
2 Kings 2:1–12
Psalm 50:1–6
2 Corinthians 4:3–6
Mark 9:2–9

General Intercessions

Let us bring our petitions before the throne of the Holy One,
presenting them through Christ to whom all glory and dominion is given.

For the church sent to witness before all peoples and nations:
May it make known to all the power and coming of our Lord Jesus Christ.

FOR THE WORLD
For nations shrouded by clouds of war and discord:
May Christ's dominion of peace dawn in splendor on their darkness.

For a world terrified by the remembrance of the atomic bomb:
May that blinding light of destruction yield to a transfiguring light of peace.

FOR THOSE OPPRESSED, AFFLICTED OR IN NEED
For lives overshadowed by the gloom of famine and disease:
May the morning star of healing and salvation rise in their hearts.

FOR THE NEEDS OF THE LOCAL COMMUNITY
For those who dedicate themselves to the service of the poor:
May their love and justice transfigure lives deprived of respect and dignity.

FOR THE CHRISTIAN ASSEMBLY
For us who have received the prophetic message of the gospel:
May we attend to it as the shining light that illumines earth's darkness.

FOR THE DEAD
For those already gone before the Lord in judgment (especially N.):
May the day of their salvation dawn in eternal radiance.

Introduction to the Lord's Prayer

Because in Christ we have received the Spirit of adoption,
as sons and daughters of God we dare to pray:

Invitation to Holy Communion

The holy gifts of God for the holy people of God:
Draw near with awe and faith, with praise and thanksgiving.

Dismissal

Giving thanks to God who has called us to share the inheritance of the saints in light,
go in peace to love and serve the Lord.

15
AUGUST

THE ASSUMPTION OF THE VIRGIN MARY INTO HEAVEN

With dancing and song, O God of the covenant,
your people Israel welcomed into their midst
the ark of your presence.
John the Baptist leaped with joy in his mother's womb
at the advent of Christ borne within Mary.

As you lifted up Mary, your chosen vessel of grace,
to share body and soul in Christ's victory over death,
so make us like her in hearing your word and
    obeying it,
that with her we may magnify your holy name.

We ask this through the Lord Jesus Christ,
the resurrection and the life,
who lives and reigns with you
in the unity of the Holy Spirit,
God for ever and ever.

In the glory of the resurrection, O God of life,
you raised up Christ to become the first fruits
    of the new creation,
and in the mystery of Mary's assumption
you have begun the great harvest of your kingdom.

Cultivate the seed already sown in our hearts,
that our hearing of the word may flower in our
    keeping of it
and may yield on the day of our own resurrection
a harvest worthy of heaven.

We ask this through the Lord Jesus Christ,
our Passover and our Peace,
who lives and reigns with you
in the unity of the Holy Spirit,
God for ever and ever.

Roman Lectionary

Vigil	Day
1 Chronicles 15:3 – 4, 15 –16; 16:1– 2	Daniel 7:9 –10, 13 –14
Psalm 132:6 – 7, 9 –10, 13 –14	Psalm 97:1– 2, 5 – 6, 9
1 Corinthians 15:54b – 57	2 Peter 1:16 –19
Luke 11:27– 28	Mark 9:2 –10

General Intercessions

Let us pray to God through Christ, the firstfruits of the resurrection,
whose victory of life we celebrate in the assumption of the Virgin Mary.

FOR THE CHURCH
For the church whose future glory is prefigured in the Virgin Mary:
Like her, may God's people magnify the Lord and bear Christ to the world.

For this world that longs to be free from war, terrorism and death:
May Christ put all these enemies under his feet and far from our lives.

FOR THOSE OPPRESSED, AFFLICTED OR IN NEED

For innocent lives devoured by the greed and violence of the powerful:
May their cause be championed by all who belong to the kingdom of God.

For believers who work to transform our society:
May they strive to lift up the lowly and fill the hungry with good things.

FOR THE NEEDS OF THE LOCAL COMMUNITY

For those who have felt the sting of death and mourn the loss of loved ones:
May the promise of immortality and the love of the community sustain them.

For those who assist expectant mothers in need, as Mary assisted Elizabeth:
May they inspire us all to mutual charity and make our hearts leap for joy.

FOR THE CHRISTIAN ASSEMBLY

For us who proclaim the victory of Christ's resurrection:
May we, like Mary, be blessed for believing the fulfillment of God's promise.

FOR THE DEAD

For those who have gone to their rest with faith in Christ's resurrection (especially N.):
May Christ come to reign in them and destroy death for ever.

Introduction to the Lord's Prayer

Let us pray for the coming of the kingdom as Jesus taught us:

Invitation to Holy Communion

Behold the living bread come down from heaven: Those who eat of it will never die.
Behold the cup of eternal life: Those who drink of it will live for ever.

Dismissal

Proclaiming the Mighty One who, in the risen Christ, has done great things for Mary and for us,
go in peace to love and serve the Lord.

14
SEPTEMBER
THE HOLY CROSS

You have highly exalted, O God,
the Christ who emptied himself,
giving the name above every name
to the one who took the form of a slave
and became obedient even to death on a cross.

Beset by danger as we journey
through this world's desert
and weakened by our own faithlessness,
we look to the One who was lifted up for our healing.
May we recognize in Jesus crucified
the Savior you sent
and exult to know how you have loved the world.

We ask this through the Lord Jesus Christ,
our Passover and our Peace,
who lives and reigns with you
in the unity of the Holy Spirit,
God for ever and ever.

Not to condemn, O God, but to save,
not to punish but to pardon,
not that we might perish
but that all might find abundant life
have you sent your only Son into the world.

In the face of life's pain,
and above all the sorrows of our history,
may we lift on high the sign of your Son's victory
and find there, for all our guilt and sin,
the healing gift of your unconquerable love.

We ask this through our Lord Jesus Christ, your Son,
who lives and reigns with you
in the unity of the Holy Spirit,
God for ever and ever.

Roman Lectionary	Revised Common Lectionary
Numbers 21:4–9	Numbers 21:4b–9
Psalm 78:1–2, 34–35, 36–37, 38	Psalm 98:1–5 or Psalm 78:1–2, 34–38
Philippians 2:6–11	1 Corinthians 1:18–24
John 3:13–17	John 3:13–17

General Intercessions

Let us offer our prayer to the God of our healing
in the name of Jesus, the crucified, whom God has highly exalted.

FOR THE CHURCH
That the people of God may not grow impatient in times of testing
but trust God's provident love to guide and sustain us on the way.

That the world may not condemn itself to war and violence
but look to the gospel of Christ for the way to healing and peace.

FOR THOSE OPPRESSED, AFFLICTED OR IN NEED
That those who hunger and thirst for justice
may find God's arm strong to save and God's servants quick to respond.

FOR THE NEEDS OF THE LOCAL COMMUNITY
That those who bear the cross of physical or emotional illness
may look on the crucified Christ as the path to healing, the pledge of exaltation.

That no one in any need or difficulty may perish through our negligence
but find among us a witness to God's love and the help of practical charity.

FOR THE CHRISTIAN ASSEMBLY
That we who gather at this table may empty ourselves
to serve and exalt, in Jesus' name, those who are seeking life and salvation.

FOR THE DEAD
That those who in life confessed Jesus as Lord (especially N.)
may now have eternal life through the victory of Christ's cross.

Introduction to the Lord's Prayer

God so loved the world that he gave his only Son,
that whoever believes in Jesus may dare to pray as he taught us:

Invitation to Holy Communion

Alleluia! Christ our paschal lamb has been sacrificed. Therefore let us keep the festival.
Blessed are those who are called to the banquet of the Lamb.

Dismissal

Confessing that Jesus is Lord, to the glory of God,
go forth in the peace of Christ.

ALL SAINTS

Great is the multitude, God of all holiness,
countless the throng you have assembled
from the rich diversity of all earth's children.
With your church in glory,
your church in this generation
lifts up our hands in prayer,
our hearts in thanksgiving and praise.

Pattern our lives on the blessedness Jesus taught,
and gather us with all the saints
into your kingdom's harvest,
that we may stand with them
and, clothed in glory, join our voices
to their hymn of thanksgiving and praise.

We ask this through our Lord Jesus Christ, your Son,
who lives and reigns with you
in the unity of the Holy Spirit,
God for ever and ever.

As one poor in spirit and gentle of heart,
your Son, O God, came to live among us,
that we might hear the charter of your kingdom
and see those words made flesh
in the mercy and peace with which he faced
insult and persecution.

As we celebrate the witness of all the saints
whose lives were shaped by the Beatitudes,
form us according to Christ's teaching
and their example,
that, having shared in the communion
of the saints on earth,
we might take our place among them
in the joy of your kingdom.

We ask this through our Lord Jesus Christ, your Son,
who lives and reigns with you
in the unity of the Holy Spirit,
God for ever and ever.

Roman Lectionary
Revelation 7:2 – 4, 9 –14
Psalm 24:1– 6
1 John 3:1– 3
Matthew 5:1–12a

General Intercessions

In communion with all the saints and in the name of Jesus,
let the incense of our prayer ascend to God, whose children we are.

INTERCESSIONS BASED ON THE BEATITUDES
That, acknowledging our complete dependence on God's gracious gifts,
we may be counted among the poor in spirit whose future is God's reign.

That those who mourn with broken hearts or spirits
may be comforted by God's compassion and consoled by God's people.

That the meek and lowly, who claim God's preferential love,
may set their hearts on the land and the future God is preparing for them.

That all who hunger and thirst for goodness in the face of human injustice
may taste God's goodness in this life and be filled in the life to come.

That, imitating God's mercy in our dealings with one another,
we may ourselves receive mercy on the day of judgment.

That the thoughts of our hearts may direct the work of our hands
and by that integrity we may behold God face to face.

That by seeking peace and pursuing it in this life,
we may, at the last day, be counted among God's angels and children.

That those persecuted for righteousness' sake
may be strengthened by the promise of the kingdom they will inherit.

Introduction to the Lord's Prayer

Because God's love has made us beloved children,
in the words of God's Son we dare to pray:

Invitation to Holy Communion

The holy gifts of God for the holy people of God:
Draw near with awe and faith, with praise and thanksgiving.

Dismissal

Giving thanks to God who has called us to share the inheritance of the saints in light,
go in peace to love and serve the Lord.

2
NOVEMBER
ALL SOULS

To destroy the shroud of death, Lord God,
and to wipe away our tears,
you promised a joyful feast on your holy mountain,
and sent your Son, the Word made flesh,
to guide us to that glory.

Bring all the faithful departed
to share the victory of the risen Christ.
Give us strength also on our earthly pilgrimage
to deny ourselves, to take up our cross
and to follow Christ,
gladly losing our lives for Jesus
and for the sake of the gospel.

We ask this through the Lord Jesus,
the resurrection and the life,
who lives and reigns with you
in the unity of the Holy Spirit,
God for ever and ever.

O God,
source of life and goal of all creation,
through the prophet's vision
you promised to destroy death forever,
and in the paschal mystery of Jesus,
the firstfruits of all who have died,
you brought that promise to fulfillment.

For all the departed who found life and light in Christ,
who took up the cross
and followed in Christ's footsteps,
grant the fulfillment of their faith at the banquet
   of life
and the joy of sharing in the salvation for which
   they waited.

We ask this through the Lord Jesus,
our Passover and our Peace,
who lives and reigns with you
in the unity of the Holy Spirit,
God for ever and ever.

Roman Lectionary
Daniel 12:1–3
Psalm 23
Romans 6:3–4, (6–7), 8–9
John 6:37–40
or any readings taken from Masses for the Dead

General Intercessions

Rejoicing in God's promised gift of salvation,
let us wait on the Lord in prayer, interceding for the living and the dead.

FOR THE CHURCH
That the people of God may gladly deny themselves in this life
for the sake of Christ and the gospel and in the hope of sharing life eternal.

That to all who have received Christ and believed in Christ's name
God may grant life without end and the light no darkness can overcome.

FOR THE WORLD
That the God of life may inspire world leaders
to destroy the violence that casts its shroud over peoples and nations.

FOR THOSE OPPRESSED, AFFLICTED OR IN NEED
That the Lord our God may wipe away the tears from all faces
and lift the burdens that oppress innocent victims of suffering.

FOR THE NEEDS OF THE LOCAL COMMUNITY
That the bereaved of our community may find consolation and strength
in our shared faith in the resurrection of Christ from the dead.

That those who work in funeral service or in bereavement ministries
may see their labor as a share in Christ's own ministry of consolation.

That the dying, who await the coming of the Lord,
may be freed from fear and filled with faith in the salvation God bestows.

FOR THE CHRISTIAN ASSEMBLY
That we who assemble here to proclaim the Lord's death until he comes
may reign with Christ when at last he destroys death forever.

FOR THE DEAD
That those who shared the eucharistic feast on earth (especially N.)
may celebrate the feast the Lord of hosts has prepared on the holy mountain.

Introduction to the Lord's Prayer

With God there is mercy and fullness of redemption;
let us pray as Jesus taught us:

◆

With longing for the coming of God's kingdom,
let us offer our prayer to the Father:

Invitation to Holy Communion

Behold the living bread come down from heaven: Those who eat of it will never die.
Behold the cup of eternal life: Those who drink of it will live for ever.

Dismissal

In the sure and certain hope of resurrection and reunion with those we love,
go in peace to love and serve the Lord.

THE DEDICATION
OF THE LATERAN BASILICA IN ROME

Eternal God,
you reveal your very being
as a communion of persons united in love,
and you show us the pattern
on which you have built us into your living temple.

On this anniversary of the dedication
of the Lateran Basilica,
fill us with consuming zeal for your house,
and through our communion with the church
of Rome,
confirm us as your universal church,
a place of welcome for all who seek you.

We ask this through our Lord Jesus Christ, your Son,
who lives and reigns with you
in the unity of the Holy Spirit,
God for ever and ever.

God most high and most holy,
whom the very heavens cannot contain,
in every generation and in every place on earth
you build a dwelling place for your Spirit
on the one foundation, Jesus Christ.

On this feast of the dedication of the cathedral of the
bishop of Rome,
Strengthen our communion with each other
and with all your people across the face of the earth.
Purify the sanctuary of our hearts,
and build us up as living stones into a holy temple.

We ask this through our Lord Jesus Christ, your Son,
who lives and reigns with you
in the unity of the Holy Spirit,
God for ever and ever.

Roman Lectionary
Ezekiel 47:1–2, 8–9, 12
Psalm 84:3–6, 8, 11
1 Corinthians 3:9c–11, 16–17
John 2:13–22
or any readings from the Common of the Dedication of a Church may be chosen

General Intercessions

Established on the foundation of Jesus Christ, and in communion with the church throughout the world,
let us pray to God who has made us a temple, living and holy.

FOR THE CHURCH
For the people of God, the living stones built into God's holy temple:
May our lives proclaim that we believe the scripture and the word of Jesus.

For the church of Rome, its bishop N. our pope, and all its people:
May the anniversary of its cathedral's dedication renew its commitment
    as a focus of unity and a model of charity for the universal church.

FOR THE WORLD
For political officials and financial leaders:
May zeal for justice consume them and transform the world with honesty and charity.

FOR THOSE OPPRESSED, AFFLICTED OR IN NEED
For all whose human dignity is exploited or destroyed:
May believers work to restore the honor due to these living temples of God.

FOR THE NEEDS OF THE LOCAL COMMUNITY
For this local church: May God broaden our vision and expand our hearts
    to grasp the gift and responsibility of communion with the universal church.

For the founders and builders of this parish church:
With zeal for prayer and service may we build on their dedicated labor.

FOR THE CHRISTIAN ASSEMBLY
For this assembly of worship and service:
From this holy temple may there flow to all the life-giving waters of healing, nourishment and peace.

FOR THE DEAD
For our deceased brothers and sisters (especially N.):
By his own resurrection may Christ raise up the temples of their bodies.

Introduction to the Lord's Prayer

Because in Christ we have received the Spirit of adoption,
as sons and daughters of God we dare to pray:

Invitation to Holy Communion

The holy gifts of God for the holy people of God:
Draw near with awe and faith, with praise and thanksgiving.

Dismissal

Giving thanks to God who has called us to share the inheritance of the saints in light,
go in peace to love and serve the Lord.

8
DECEMBER
THE IMMACULATE CONCEPTION OF THE VIRGIN MARY

Creator God, in your gracious providence
time runs to fulfillment and perfection in you.
Here in the depths of Advent,
we herald the paschal spring,
the immaculate conception of the Virgin Mary,
the first shoot gives unfailing promise
  of the flower still to come.

Let the fullness of your grace, which enfolded Mary,
kindle in our hearts the light of hope
and the warmth of love.

We ask this through our Lord Jesus Christ,
who was, who is and who is to come,
your Son who lives and reigns with you
in the unity of the Holy Spirit,
God for ever and ever.

Lord God of all creation,
from the first moment of our disobedience
you promised redemption,
and from the first moment of her conception,
you fashioned the Virgin Mary full of grace,
to be the image of the church,
the woman of faith,
the model of discipleship.

As you chose her to be mother of the Redeemer
and destined us for adoption through her Son,
place on our lips her gracious acceptance of your will,
bestir our hearts to trust in your promise
and bring forth in our lives
her witness of obedient faith.

We ask this through our Lord Jesus Christ,
who was, who is and who is to come,
your Son who lives and reigns with you
in the unity of the Holy Spirit,
God for ever and ever.

Roman Lectionary
Genesis 3:9–15, 20
Psalm 98
Ephesians 1:3–6, 11–12
Luke 1:26–38

General Intercessions

With the obedient faith of Mary as our model,
let us pray to God who accomplishes all things according to his counsel and will.

FOR THE CHURCH

That the church may embrace the mystery of God's will as Mary did,
with faith in the God for whom all things are possible.

FOR THE WORLD

That peoples divided by enmity may find the path to peace
through the intercession of the mother of our Redeemer.

FOR THOSE OPPRESSED, AFFLICTED OR IN NEED

That those whose sins have made them fearful or ashamed
may find the hope of a new beginning in the Messiah born of Mary.

FOR THE NEEDS OF THE LOCAL COMMUNITY

That expectant parents may find this Advent a season of joyful anticipation,
a time to join Mary in praising the God who does marvelous deeds.

FOR THE CHRISTIAN ASSEMBLY

That we who were adopted in Christ the Beloved by God's gracious choice
may live holy and blameless lives as we look forward to his coming.

FOR THE DEAD

That those gone before us in faith (especially N.)
may obtain the inheritance for which they were destined in Christ.

Introduction to the Lord's Prayer

Let us pray for the coming of the kingdom as Jesus taught us:

Invitation to Holy Communion

Behold the Lord whose advent we await, who will come with glory on the day of judgment.
Blessed are those who are called to the banquet of the Lamb.

Dismissal

Go forth in peace to prepare the way of the Lord.

Calendar of Sundays and Feasts According to the Roman Calendar, 1997–2015

SUNDAY/FEAST DAY	1997 YEAR B	1998 YEAR C	1999 YEAR A
1st Sunday of Advent	December 1, 1996	November 30, 1997	November 29, 1998
2nd Sunday of Advent	December 8, 1996	December 7, 1997	December 6, 1998
Immaculate Conception, December 8	December 9, 1996[+]	Monday	Tuesday
3rd Sunday of Advent	December 15, 1996	December 14, 1997	December 13, 1998
4th Sunday of Advent	December 22, 1996	December 21, 1997	December 20, 1998
Christmas, December 25	Wednesday	Thursday	Friday
Holy Family	December 29, 1996	December 28, 1997	December 27, 1998
Mary, Mother of God, January 1	Wednesday	Thursday	Friday
Epiphany	January 5, 1997	January 4, 1998	January 3, 1999
Baptism of the Lord	January 12, 1997	January 11, 1998	January 10, 1992
2nd Sunday in Ordinary Time	January 19	January 18	January 17
3rd Sunday in Ordinary Time	January 26	January 25	January 24
4th Sunday in Ordinary Time	_____	February 1	January 31
Presentation of the Lord, February 2	Sunday	Monday	Tuesday
5th Sunday in Ordinary Time	February 9	February 8	February 7
6th Sunday in Ordinary Time	_____	February 15	February 14
7th Sunday in Ordinary Time	_____	February 22	_____
8th Sunday in Ordinary Time	_____	_____	_____
9th Sunday in Ordinary Time	_____	_____	_____
Ash Wednesday	February 12	February 25	February 17
1st Sunday of Lent	February 16	March 1	February 21
2nd Sunday of Lent	February 23	March 8	February 28
3rd Sunday of Lent	March 2	March 15	March 7
4th Sunday of Lent	March 9	March 22	March 14
5th Sunday of Lent	March 16	March 29	March 21
Passion (Palm) Sunday	March 23	April 5	March 28
■ Joseph, Husband of Mary, March 19	Wednesday	Thursday	Friday
■ Annunciation, March 25	April 7[+]	Wednesday	Thursday

+ This solemnity has been transferred to this date.

SUNDAY/FEAST DAY	1997 YEAR B	1998 YEAR C	1999 YEAR A
Holy Thursday	March 27	April 9	April 1
Good Friday	March 28	April 10	April 2
Easter Sunday	March 30	April 12	April 4
2nd Sunday of Easter	April 6	April 19	April 11
3rd Sunday of Easter	April 13	April 26	April 18
4th Sunday of Easter	April 20	May 3	April 25
5th Sunday of Easter	April 27	May 10	May 2
6th Sunday of Easter	May 4	May 17	May 9
Ascension	May 8	May 21	May 13
7th Sunday of Easter	May 11	May 24	May 16
Pentecost	May 18	May 31	May 23
Trinity Sunday	May 25	June 7	May 30
Body and Blood of Christ	June 1	June 14	June 6
Sacred Heart	June 6	June 19	June 11
9th Sunday in Ordinary Time	————	————	————
10th Sunday in Ordinary Time	June 8	————	————
11th Sunday in Ordinary Time	June 15	————	June 13
12th Sunday in Ordinary Time	June 22	June 21	June 20
Birth of John the Baptist, June 24	Tuesday	Wednesday	Thursday
13th Sunday in Ordinary Time	————	June 28	June 27
Peter and Paul, Apostles, June 29	Sunday	Monday	Tuesday
Independence Day, July 4	Friday	Saturday	* *
14th Sunday in Ordinary Time	July 6	July 5	July 4
15th Sunday in Ordinary Time	July 13	July 12	July 11
16th Sunday in Ordinary Time	July 20	July 19	July 18
17th Sunday in Ordinary Time	July 27	July 26	July 25
18th Sunday in Ordinary Time	August 3	August 2	August 1
Transfiguration, August 6	Wednesday	Thursday	Friday

* * When Independence Day falls on Sunday, the special Votive Mass texts are not used.

SUNDAY/FEAST DAY	1997 YEAR B	1998 YEAR C	1999 YEAR A
19th Sunday in Ordinary Time	August 10	August 9	August 8
Assumption, August 15	Friday	Saturday	Sunday
20th Sunday in Ordinary Time	August 17	August 16	———
21st Sunday in Ordinary Time	August 24	August 23	August 22
22nd Sunday in Ordinary Time	August 31	August 30	August 29
Labor Day	September 1	September 7	September 6
23rd Sunday in Ordinary Time	September 7	September 6	September 5
Triumph of the Cross, September 14	Sunday	Monday	Tuesday
24th Sunday in Ordinary Time	———	September 13	September 12
25th Sunday in Ordinary Time	September 21	September 20	September 19
26th Sunday in Ordinary Time	September 28	September 27	September 26
27th Sunday in Ordinary Time	October 5	October 4	October 3
28th Sunday in Ordinary Time	October 12	October 11	October 10
29th Sunday in Ordinary Time	October 19	October 18	October 17
30th Sunday in Ordinary Time	October 26	October 25	October 24
31st Sunday in Ordinary Time	———	———	October 31
All Saints, November 1	Saturday	Sunday	Monday
All Souls, November 2	Sunday	Monday	Tuesday
32nd Sunday in Ordinary Time	———	November 8	November 7
Dedication of St. John Lateran, November 9	Sunday	Monday	Tuesday
33rd Sunday in Ordinary Time	November 16	November 15	November 14
Christ the King	November 23	November 22	November 21
Thanksgiving	November 27	November 26	November 25

◆

SUNDAY/FEAST DAY	2000 YEAR B	2001 YEAR C	2002 YEAR A
1st Sunday of Advent	November 28, 1999	December 3, 2000	December 2, 2001
2nd Sunday of Advent	December 5, 1999	December 10, 2000	December 9, 2001

SUNDAY/FEAST DAY	2000 YEAR B	2001 YEAR C	2002 YEAR A
Immaculate Conception, December 8	Wednesday	Friday	Saturday
3rd Sunday of Advent	December 12, 1999	December 17, 2000	December 16, 2001
4th Sunday of Advent	December 19, 1999	December 24, 2000	December 23, 2001
Christmas, December 25	Saturday	Monday	Tuesday
Holy Family	December 26, 1999	December 31, 2000	December 30, 2001
Mary, Mother of God, January 1	Saturday	Monday	Tuesday
Epiphany	January 2, 2000	January 7, 2001	January 6, 2002
Baptism of the Lord	January 9, 2000	January 8, 2001*	January 13, 2002
2nd Sunday in Ordinary Time	Jan 16	January 14	January 20
3rd Sunday in Ordinary Time	January 23	January 21	January 27
4th Sunday in Ordinary Time	January 30	January 28	February 3
Presentation of the Lord, February 2	Wednesday	Friday	Saturday
5th Sunday in Ordinary Time	February 6	February 4	February 10
6th Sunday in Ordinary Time	February 13	February 11	————
7th Sunday in Ordinary Time	February 20	February 18	————
8th Sunday in Ordinary Time	February 27	February 25	————
9th Sunday in Ordinary Time	March 5	————	————
Ash Wednesday	March 8	February 28	February 13
1st Sunday of Lent	March 12	March 4	February 17
2nd Sunday of Lent	March 19	March 11	February 24
3rd Sunday of Lent	March 26	March 18	March 3
4th Sunday of Lent	April 2	March 25	March 10
5th Sunday of Lent	April 9	April 1	March 17
Passion (Palm) Sunday	April 16	April 8	March 24
■ Joseph, Husband of Mary, March 19	March 20+	Monday	Tuesday
■ Annunciation, March 25	Saturday	March 26+	April 8+
Holy Thursday	April 20	April 12	March 28
Good Friday	April 21	April 13	March 29

* This feast is celebrated this year on a weekday.   + This solemnity has been transferred to this date.

SUNDAY/FEAST DAY	2000 YEAR B	2001 YEAR C	2002 YEAR A
Easter Sunday	April 23	April 15	March 31
2nd Sunday of Easter	April 30	April 22	April 7
3rd Sunday of Easter	May 7	April 29	April 14
4th Sunday of Easter	May 14	May 6	April 21
5th Sunday of Easter	May 21	May 13	April 28
6th Sunday of Easter	May 28	May 20	May 5
Ascension	June 1	May 24	May 9
7th Sunday of Easter	June 4	May 27	May 12
Pentecost	June 11	June 3	May 19
Trinity Sunday	June 18	June 10	May 26
Body and Blood of Christ	June 25	June 17	June 2
Sacred Heart	June 30	June 22	June 7
9th Sunday in Ordinary Time	_____	_____	_____
10th Sunday in Ordinary Time	_____	_____	June 9
11th Sunday in Ordinary Time	_____	_____	June 16
12th Sunday in Ordinary Time	_____	_____	June 23
Birth of John the Baptist, June 24	Saturday	Sunday	Monday
13th Sunday in Ordinary Time	July 2	July 1	June 30
Peter and Paul, Apostles, June 29	Thursday	Friday	Saturday
Independence Day, July 4	Tuesday	Wednesday	Thursday
14th Sunday in Ordinary Time	July 9	July 8	July 7
15th Sunday in Ordinary Time	July 16	July 15	July 14
16th Sunday in Ordinary Time	July 23	July 22	July 21
17th Sunday in Ordinary Time	July 30	July 29	July 28
18th Sunday in Ordinary Time	_____	August 5	August 4
Transfiguration, August 6	Sunday	Monday	Tuesday
19th Sunday in Ordinary Time	August 13	August 12	August 11
Assumption, August 15	Tuesday	Wednesday	Thursday
20th Sunday in Ordinary Time	August 20	August 19	August 18

SUNDAY/FEAST DAY	2000 YEAR B	2001 YEAR C	2002 YEAR A
21st Sunday in Ordinary Time	August 27	August 26	August 25
22nd Sunday in Ordinary Time	September 3	September 2	September 1
Labor Day	September 4	September 3	September 2
23rd Sunday in Ordinary Time	September 10	September 9	September 8
Triumph of the Cross, September 14	Thursday	Friday	Saturday
24th Sunday in Ordinary Time	September 17	September 16	September 15
25th Sunday in Ordinary Time	September 24	September 23	September 22
26th Sunday in Ordinary Time	October 1	September 30	September 29
27th Sunday in Ordinary Time	October 8	October 7	October 6
28th Sunday in Ordinary Time	October 15	October 14	October 13
29th Sunday in Ordinary Time	October 22	October 21	October 20
30th Sunday in Ordinary Time	October 29	October 28	October 27
31st Sunday in Ordinary Time	November 5	November 4	November 3
All Saints, November 1	Wednesday	Thursday	Friday
All Souls, November 2	Thursday	Friday	Saturday
32nd Sunday in Ordinary Time	November 12	November 11	November 10
Dedication of St. John Lateran, November 9	Thursday	Friday	Saturday
33rd Sunday in Ordinary Time	November 19	November 18	November 17
Christ the King	November 26	November 25	November 24
Thanksgiving	November 23	November 22	November 21

◆

SUNDAY/FEAST DAY	2003 YEAR B	2004 YEAR C	2005 YEAR A
1st Sunday of Advent	December 1, 2002	November 30, 2003	November 28, 2004
2nd Sunday of Advent	December 8, 2002	December 7, 2003	December 5, 2004
Immaculate Conception, December 8	December 9, 2002[+]	Monday	Wednesday

+ This solemnity has been transferred to this date.

SUNDAY/FEAST DAY	2003 YEAR B	2004 YEAR C	2005 YEAR A
3rd Sunday of Advent	December 15, 2002	December 14, 2003	December 12, 2004
4th Sunday of Advent	December 22, 2002	December 21, 2003	December 19, 2004
Christmas, December 25	Wednesday	Thursday	Saturday
Holy Family	December 29, 2002	December 28, 2003	December 26, 2004
Mary, Mother of God, January 1	Wednesday	Thursday	Saturday
Epiphany	January 5, 2003	January 4, 2004	January 2, 2005
Baptism of the Lord	January 12, 2003	January 11, 2004	January 9, 2005
2nd Sunday in Ordinary Time	January 19	January 18	January 16
3rd Sunday in Ordinary Time	January 26	January 25	January 23
4th Sunday in Ordinary Time	_____	February 1	January 30
Presentation of the Lord, February 2	Sunday	Monday	Wednesday
5th Sunday in Ordinary Time	February 9	February 8	February 6
6th Sunday in Ordinary Time	February 16	February 15	_____
7th Sunday in Ordinary Time	February 23	February 22	_____
8th Sunday in Ordinary Time	March 2	_____	_____
9th Sunday in Ordinary Time	_____	_____	_____
Ash Wednesday	March 5	February 25	February 9
1st Sunday of Lent	March 9	February 29	February 13
2nd Sunday of Lent	March 16	March 7	February 20
3rd Sunday of Lent	March 23	March 14	February 27
4th Sunday of Lent	March 30	March 21	March 6
5th Sunday of Lent	April 6	March 28	March 13
Passion (Palm) Sunday	April 13	April 4	March 20
■ Joseph, Husband of Mary, March 19	Wednesday	Friday	Saturday
■ Annunciation, March 25	Tuesday	Thursday	April 4+
Holy Thursday	April 17	April 8	March 24
Good Friday	April 18	April 9	March 25
Easter Sunday	April 20	April 11	March 27

+ This solemnity has been transferred to this date.

SUNDAY/FEAST DAY	2003 YEAR B	2004 YEAR C	2005 YEAR A
2nd Sunday of Easter	April 27	April 18	April 3
3rd Sunday of Easter	May 4	April 25	April 10
4th Sunday of Easter	May 11	May 2	April 17
5th Sunday of Easter	May 18	May 9	April 24
6th Sunday of Easter	May 25	May 16	May 1
Ascension	May 29	May 20	May 5
7th Sunday of Easter	June 1	May 23	May 8
Pentecost	June 8	May 30	May 15
Trinity Sunday	June 15	June 6	May 22
Body and Blood of Christ	June 22	June 13	May 29
Sacred Heart	June 27	June 18	June 3
9th Sunday in Ordinary Time	_____	_____	_____
10th Sunday in Ordinary Time	_____	_____	June 5
11th Sunday in Ordinary Time	_____	_____	June 12
12th Sunday in Ordinary Time	_____	June 20	June 19
Birth of John the Baptist, June 24	Tuesday	Thursday	Friday
13th Sunday in Ordinary Time	_____	June 27	June 26
Peter and Paul, Apostles, June 29	Sunday	Tuesday	Wednesday
Independence Day, July 4	Friday	* *	Monday
14th Sunday in Ordinary Time	July 6	July 4	July 3
15th Sunday in Ordinary Time	July 13	July 11	July 10
16th Sunday in Ordinary Time	July 20	July 18	July 17
17th Sunday in Ordinary Time	July 27	July 25	July 24
18th Sunday in Ordinary Time	August 3	August 1	July 31
Transfiguration, August 6	Wednesday	Friday	Saturday
19th Sunday in Ordinary Time	August 10	August 8	August 7
Assumption, August 15	Friday	Sunday	Monday
20th Sunday in Ordinary Time	August 17	_____	August 14

* * When Independence Day falls on Sunday, the special Votive Mass texts are not used.

◆

SUNDAY/FEAST DAY	2003 YEAR B	2004 YEAR C	2005 YEAR A
21st Sunday in Ordinary Time	August 24	August 22	August 21
22nd Sunday in Ordinary Time	August 31	August 29	August 28
Labor Day	September 1	September 6	September 5
23rd Sunday in Ordinary Time	September 7	September 5	September 4
Triumph of the Cross, September 14	Sunday	Tuesday	Wednesday
24th Sunday in Ordinary Time	_____	September 12	September 11
25th Sunday in Ordinary Time	September 21	September 19	September 18
26th Sunday in Ordinary Time	September 28	September 26	September 25
27th Sunday in Ordinary Time	October 5	October 3	October 2
28th Sunday in Ordinary Time	October 12	October 10	October 9
29th Sunday in Ordinary Time	October 19	October 17	October 16
30th Sunday in Ordinary Time	October 26	October 24	October 23
31st Sunday in Ordinary Time	_____	October 31	October 30
All Saints, November 1	Saturday	Monday	Tuesday
All Souls, November 2	Sunday	Tues	Wednesday
32nd Sunday in Ordinary Time	_____	November 7	November 6
Dedication of St. John Lateran, November 9	Sunday	Tuesday	Wednesday
33rd Sunday in Ordinary Time	November 16	November 14	November 13
Christ the King	November 23	November 21	November 20
Thanksgiving	November 27	November 25	November 24

◆

SUNDAY/FEAST DAY	2006 YEAR B	2007 YEAR C	2008 YEAR A
1st Sunday of Advent	November 27, 2005	December 3, 2006	December 2, 2007
2nd Sunday of Advent	December 4, 2005	December 10, 2006	December 9, 2007
Immaculate Conception, December 8	Thursday	Friday	Saturday
3rd Sunday of Advent	December 11, 2005	December 17, 2006	December 16, 2007

◆

SUNDAY/FEAST DAY	2006 YEAR B	2007 YEAR C	2008 YEAR A
4th Sunday of Advent	December 18, 2005	December 24, 2006	December 23, 2007
Christmas, December 25	Sunday	Monday	Tuesday
Holy Family	December 30, 2005+	December 31, 2006	December 30, 2007
Mary, Mother of God, January 1	Sunday	Monday	Tuesday
Epiphany	January 8, 2006	January 7, 2007	January 6, 2008
Baptism of the Lord	January 9, 2006+	January 8, 2007+	January 13, 2008
2nd Sunday in Ordinary Time	January 15	January 14	January 20
3rd Sunday in Ordinary Time	January 22	January 21	January 27
4th Sunday in Ordinary Time	January 29	January 28	February 3
Presentation of the Lord, February 2	Thursday	Friday	Saturday
5th Sunday in Ordinary Time	February 5	February 4	———
6th Sunday in Ordinary Time	February 12	February 11	———
7th Sunday in Ordinary Time	February 19	February 18	———
8th Sunday in Ordinary Time	February 26	———	———
9th Sunday in Ordinary Time	———	———	———
Ash Wednesday	March 1	February 21	February 6
1st Sunday of Lent	March 5	February 25	February 10
2nd Sunday of Lent	March 12	March 4	February 17
3rd Sunday of Lent	March 19	March 11	February 24
4th Sunday of Lent	March 26	March 18	March 2
5th Sunday of Lent	April 2	March 25	March 9
Passion (Palm) Sunday	April 9	April 1	March 16
■ Joseph, Husband of Mary, March 19	March 20+	Monday	March 31+
■ Annunciation, March 25	Saturday	March 26+	April 1+
Holy Thursday	April 13	April 5	March 20
Good Friday	April 14	April 6	March 21
Easter Sunday	April 16	April 8	March 23
2nd Sunday of Easter	April 23	April 15	March 30

+ This solemnity has been transferred to this date.

SUNDAY/FEAST DAY	2006 YEAR B	2007 YEAR C	2008 YEAR A
3rd Sunday of Easter	April 30	April 22	April 6
4th Sunday of Easter	May 7	April 29	April 13
5th Sunday of Easter	May 14	May 6	April 20
6th Sunday of Easter	May 21	May 13	April 27
Ascension	May 25	May 17	May 1
7th Sunday of Easter	May 28	May 20	May 4
Pentecost	June 4	May 27	May 11
Trinity Sunday	June 11	June 3	May 18
Body and Blood of Christ	June 18	June 10	May 25
Sacred Heart	June 23	June 15	May 30
9th Sunday in Ordinary Time	_____	_____	June 1
10th Sunday in Ordinary Time	_____	_____	June 8
11th Sunday in Ordinary Time	_____	June 17	June 15
12th Sunday in Ordinary Time	June 25	_____	June 22
Birth of John the Baptist, June 24	Saturday	Sunday	Tuesday
13th Sunday in Ordinary Time	July 2	July 1	_____
Peter and Paul, Apostles, June 29	Thursday	Friday	Sunday
Independence Day, July 4	Tuesday	Wednesday	Friday
14th Sunday in Ordinary Time	July 9	July 8	July 6
15th Sunday in Ordinary Time	July 16	July 15	July 13
16th Sunday in Ordinary Time	July 23	July 22	July 20
17th Sunday in Ordinary Time	July 30	July 29	July 27
18th Sunday in Ordinary Time	_____	August 5	August 3
Transfiguration, August 6	Sunday	Monday	Wednesday
19th Sunday in Ordinary Time	August 13	August 12	August 10
Assumption, August 15	Tuesday	Wednesday	Friday
20th Sunday in Ordinary Time	August 20	August 19	August 17
21st Sunday in Ordinary Time	August 27	August 26	August 24
22nd Sunday in Ordinary Time	September 3	September 2	August 31

SUNDAY/FEAST DAY	2006 YEAR B	2007 YEAR C	2008 YEAR A
Labor Day	September 4	September 3	September 1
23rd Sunday in Ordinary Time	September 10	September 9	September 7
Triumph of the Cross, September 14	Thursday	Friday	Sunday
24th Sunday in Ordinary Time	September 17	September 16	———
25th Sunday in Ordinary Time	September 24	September 23	September 21
26th Sunday in Ordinary Time	October 1	September 30	September 28
27th Sunday in Ordinary Time	October 8	October 7	October 5
28th Sunday in Ordinary Time	October 15	October 14	October 12
29th Sunday in Ordinary Time	October 22	October 21	October 19
30th Sunday in Ordinary Time	October 29	October 28	October 26
31st Sunday in Ordinary Time	November 5	November 4	———
All Saints, November 1	Wednesday	Thursday	Saturday
All Souls, November 2	Thursday	Friday	Sunday
32nd Sunday in Ordinary Time	November 12	November 11	———
Dedication of St. John Lateran, November 9	Thursday	Friday	Sunday
33rd Sunday in Ordinary Time	November 19	November 18	November 16
Christ the King	November 26	November 25	November 23
Thanksgiving	November 23	November 22	November 20

SUNDAY/FEAST DAY	2009 YEAR B	2010 YEAR C	2011 YEAR A
1st Sunday of Advent	November 30, 2008	November 29, 2009	November 28, 2010
2nd Sunday of Advent	December 7, 2008	December 6, 2009	December 5, 2010
Immaculate Conception, December 8	Monday	Tuesday	Wednesday
3rd Sunday of Advent	December 14, 2008	December 13, 2009	December 12, 2010
4th Sunday of Advent	December 21, 2008	December 20, 2009	December 19, 2010
Christmas, December 25	Thursday	Friday	Saturday

SUNDAY/FEAST DAY	2009 YEAR B	2010 YEAR C	2011 YEAR A
Holy Family	December 28, 2008	December 27, 2009	December 26, 2010
Mary, Mother of God, January 1	Thursday	Friday	Saturday
Epiphany	January 4, 2009	January 3, 2010	January 2, 2011
Baptism of the Lord	January 11, 2009	January 10, 2010	January 9, 2011
2nd Sunday in Ordinary Time	January 18	January 17	January 16
3rd Sunday in Ordinary Time	January 25	January 24	January 23
4th Sunday in Ordinary Time	February 1	January 31	January 30
Presentation of the Lord, February 2	Monday	Tuesday	Wednesday
5th Sunday in Ordinary Time	February 8	February 7	February 6
6th Sunday in Ordinary Time	February 15	February 14	February 13
7th Sunday in Ordinary Time	February 22	_____	February 20
8th Sunday in Ordinary Time	_____	_____	February 27
9th Sunday in Ordinary Time	_____	_____	March 6
Ash Wednesday	February 25	February 17	March 9
1st Sunday of Lent	March 1	February 21	March 13
2nd Sunday of Lent	March 8	February 28	March 20
3rd Sunday of Lent	March 15	March 7	March 27
4th Sunday of Lent	March 22	March 14	April 3
5th Sunday of Lent	March 29	March 21	April 10
Passion (Palm) Sunday	April 5	March 28	April 17
▪ Joseph, Husband of Mary, March 19	Thursday	Friday	Saturday
▪ Annunciation, March 25	Wednesday	Thursday	Friday
Holy Thursday	April 9	April 1	April 21
Good Friday	April 10	April 2	April 22
Easter Sunday	April 12	April 4	April 24
2nd Sunday of Easter	April 19	April 11	May 1
3rd Sunday of Easter	April 26	April 18	May 8
4th Sunday of Easter	May 3	April 25	May 15
5th Sunday of Easter	May 10	May 2	May 22

SUNDAY/FEAST DAY	2009 YEAR B	2010 YEAR C	2011 YEAR A
6th Sunday of Easter	May 17	May 9	May 29
Ascension	May 21	May 13	June 2
7th Sunday of Easter	May 24	May 16	June 5
Pentecost	May 31	May 23	June 12
Trinity Sunday	June 7	May 30	June 19
Body and Blood of Christ	June 14	June 6	June 26
Sacred Heart	June 19	June 11	July 1
9th Sunday in Ordinary Time	_____	_____	_____
10th Sunday in Ordinary Time	_____	_____	_____
11th Sunday in Ordinary Time	_____	June 13	_____
12th Sunday in Ordinary Time	June 21	June 20	_____
Birth of John the Baptist, June 24	Wednesday	Thursday	Friday
13th Sunday in Ordinary Time	June 28	June 27	_____
Peter and Paul, Apostles, June 29	Monday	Tuesday	Wednesday
Independence Day, July 4	Saturday	* *	Monday
14th Sunday in Ordinary Time	July 5	July 4	July 3
15th Sunday in Ordinary Time	July 12	July 11	July 10
16th Sunday in Ordinary Time	July 19	July 18	July 17
17th Sunday in Ordinary Time	July 26	July 25	July 24
18th Sunday in Ordinary Time	August 2	August 1	July 31
Transfiguration, August 6	Thursday	Friday	Saturday
19th Sunday in Ordinary Time	August 9	August 8	August 7
Assumption, August 15	Saturday	Sunday	Monday
20th Sunday in Ordinary Time	August 16	_____	August 14
21st Sunday in Ordinary Time	August 23	August 22	August 21
22nd Sunday in Ordinary Time	August 30	August 29	August 28
Labor Day	September 7	September 6	September 5
23rd Sunday in Ordinary Time	September 6	September 5	September 4

* * When Independence Day falls on Sunday, the special Votive Mass texts are not used.

SUNDAY/FEAST DAY	2009 YEAR B	2010 YEAR C	2011 YEAR A
Triumph of the Cross, September 14	Monday	Tuesday	Wednesday
24th Sunday in Ordinary Time	September 13	September 12	September 11
25th Sunday in Ordinary Time	September 20	September 19	September 18
26th Sunday in Ordinary Time	September 27	September 26	September 25
27th Sunday in Ordinary Time	October 4	October 3	October 2
28th Sunday in Ordinary Time	October 11	October 10	October 9
29th Sunday in Ordinary Time	October 18	October 17	October 16
30th Sunday in Ordinary Time	October 25	October 24	October 23
31st Sunday in Ordinary Time	_____	October 31	October 30
All Saints, November 1	Sunday	Monday	Tuesday
All Souls, November 2	Monday	Tuesday	Wednesday
32nd Sunday in Ordinary Time	November 8	November 7	November 6
Dedication of St. John Lateran, November 9	Monday	Tuesday	Wednesday
33rd Sunday in Ordinary Time	November 15	November 14	November 13
Christ the King	November 22	November 21	November 20
Thanksgiving	November 26	November 25	November 24

◆

SUNDAY/FEAST DAY	2012 YEAR B	2013 YEAR C	2014 YEAR A
1st Sunday of Advent	November 27, 2011	December 2, 2012	December 1, 2013
2nd Sunday of Advent	December 4, 2011	December 9, 2012	December 8, 2013
Immaculate Conception, December 8	Thursday	Saturday	December 9, 2013+
3rd Sunday of Advent	December 11, 2011	December 16, 2012	December 15, 2013
4th Sunday of Advent	December 18, 2011	December 23, 2012	December 22, 2013
Christmas, December 25	Sunday	Tuesday	Wednesday
Holy Family	December 30, 2011+	December 30, 2012	December 29, 2013

+ This solemnity has been transferred to this date.

SUNDAY/FEAST DAY	2012 YEAR B	2013 YEAR C	2014 YEAR A
Mary, Mother of God, January 1	Sunday	Tuesday	Wednesday
Epiphany	January 8, 2012	January 6, 2013	January 5, 2014
Baptism of the Lord	January 9, 2012+	January 13, 2013	January 12, 2014
2nd Sunday in Ordinary Time	January 15	January 20	January 19
3rd Sunday in Ordinary Time	January 22	January 27	January 26
4th Sunday in Ordinary Time	January 29	February 3	————
Presentation of the Lord, February 2	Thursday	Saturday	Sunday
5th Sunday in Ordinary Time	February 5	February 10	February 9
6th Sunday in Ordinary Time	February 12	————	February16
7th Sunday in Ordinary Time	February 19	————	February 23
8th Sunday in Ordinary Time	————	————	March 2
9th Sunday in Ordinary Time	————	————.	————
Ash Wednesday	February 22	February 13	March 5
1st Sunday of Lent	February 26	February 17	March 9
2nd Sunday of Lent	March 4	February 24	March 16
3rd Sunday of Lent	March 11	March 3	March 23
4th Sunday of Lent	March 18	March 10	March 30
5th Sunday of Lent	March 25	March 17	April 6
Passion (Palm) Sunday	April 1	March 24	April 13
▪ Joseph, Husband of Mary, March 19	Monday	Tuesday	Wednesday
▪ Annunciation, March 25	March 26+	April 8+	Tuesday
Holy Thursday	April 5	March 28	April 17
Good Friday	April 6	March 29	April 18
Easter Sunday	April 8	March 31	April 20
2nd Sunday of Easter	April 15	April 7	April 27
3rd Sunday of Easter	April 22	April 14	May 4
4th Sunday of Easter	April 29	April 21	May 11
5th Sunday of Easter	May 6	April 28	May 18

+ This solemnity has been transferred to this date.

SUNDAY/FEAST DAY	2012 YEAR B	2013 YEAR C	2014 YEAR A
6th Sunday of Easter	May 13	May 5	May 25
Ascension	May 17	May 9	May 29
7th Sunday of Easter	May 20	May 12	June 1
Pentecost	May 27	May 19	June 8
Trinity Sunday	June 3	May 26	June 15
Body and Blood of Christ	June 10	June 2	June 22
Sacred Heart	June 15	June 7	June 27
9th Sunday in Ordinary Time	_____	_____	_____
10th Sunday in Ordinary Time	_____	June 9	_____
11th Sunday in Ordinary Time	June 17	June 16	_____
12th Sunday in Ordinary Time	_____	June 23	_____
Birth of John the Baptist, June 24	Sunday	Monday	Tuesday
13th Sunday in Ordinary Time	July 1	June 30	_____
Peter and Paul, Apostles, June 29	Friday	Saturday	Sunday
Independence Day, July 4	Wednesday	Thursday	Friday
14th Sunday in Ordinary Time	July 8	July 7	July 6
15th Sunday in Ordinary Time	July 15	July 14	July 13
16th Sunday in Ordinary Time	July 22	July 21	July 20
17th Sunday in Ordinary Time	July 29	July 28	July 27
18th Sunday in Ordinary Time	August 5	August 4	August 3
Transfiguration, August 6	Monday	Tuesday	Wednesday
19th Sunday in Ordinary Time	August 12	August 11	August 10
Assumption, August 15	Wednesday	Thursday	Friday
20th Sunday in Ordinary Time	August 19	August 18	August 17
21st Sunday in Ordinary Time	August 26	August 25	August 24
22nd Sunday in Ordinary Time	September 2	September 1	August 31
Labor Day	September 3	September 2	September 8
23rd Sunday in Ordinary Time	September 9	September 8	September 7
Triumph of the Cross, September 14	Friday	Saturday	Sunday

◆

SUNDAY/FEAST DAY	2012 YEAR B	2013 YEAR C	2014 YEAR A
24th Sunday in Ordinary Time	September 16	September 15	————
25th Sunday in Ordinary Time	September 23	September 22	September 21
26th Sunday in Ordinary Time	September 30	September 29	September 28
27th Sunday in Ordinary Time	October 7	October 6	October 5
28th Sunday in Ordinary Time	October 14	October 13	October 12
29th Sunday in Ordinary Time	October 21	October 20	October 19
30th Sunday in Ordinary Time	October 28	October 27	October 26
31st Sunday in Ordinary Time	November 4	November 3	————
All Saints, November 1	Thursday	Friday	Saturday
All Souls, November 2	Friday	Saturday	Sunday
32nd Sunday in Ordinary Time	November 11	November 10	————
Dedication of St. John Lateran, November 9	Friday	Saturday	Sunday
33rd Sunday in Ordinary Time	November 18	November 17	November 16
Christ the King	November 25	November 24	November 23
Thanksgiving	November 22	November 26	November 27

◆

Titles and Dates of Sundays and Special Days According to the *Revised Common Lectionary*

SEASON OF ADVENT

First Sunday of Advent — Sunday between November 27 and December 3

Second Sunday of Advent — Sunday between December 4 and December 10

Third Sunday of Advent — Sunday between December 11 and December 17

Fourth Sunday of Advent — Sunday between December 18 and December 24

SEASON OF CHRISTMAS

Nativity of the Lord
(Christmas Day) — December 25

First Sunday after Christmas — Sunday between December 26 and January 1

New Year's Day — January 1

Second Sunday after Christmas — Sunday between January 2 and January 5

SEASON OF EPIPHANY

Epiphany of the Lord — January 6 or First Sunday in January

First Sunday after the Epiphany [1] (Baptism of the Lord) — Sunday between January 7 and January 13

Second Sunday after the Epiphany [2] — Sunday between January 14 and January 20

Third Sunday after the Epiphany [3] — Sunday between January 21 and January 27

Fourth Sunday after the Epiphany [4] — Sunday between January 28 and February 3

Fifth Sunday after the Epiphany [5] — Sunday between February 4 and February 10

Sixth Sunday after the Epiphany [6] (Proper 1, except when this Sunday is the Last Sunday after the Epiphany) — Sunday between February 11 and February 17

Seventh Sunday after the Epiphany [7] (Proper 2, except when this Sunday is the Last Sunday after the Epiphany — Sunday between February 18 and February 24

Eighth Sunday after the Epiphany [8] (Proper 3, except when this Sunday is the last Sunday after the Epiphany)

Sunday between February 25 and February 29

Ninth Sunday after the Epiphany [9] (Proper 3, for Churches that do not observe the Last Sunday after the Epiphany with Transfiguration readings)

Sunday between March 1 and March 7

Last Sunday after the Epiphany
(Transfiguration Sunday)

SEASON OF LENT

Ash Wednesday

First Sunday in Lent

Second Sunday in Lent

Third Sunday in Lent

Fourth Sunday in Lent

Fifth Sunday in Lent

Sixth Sunday in Lent (Passion Sunday or Palm Sunday)

Holy Week
    Monday of Holy Week
    Tuesday of Holy Week
    Wednesday of Holy Week
    Holy Thursday
    Good Friday
    Holy Saturday

SEASON OF EEASTER

Resurrection of the Lord
    Easter Vigil
    Easter Day

Second Sunday of Easter

Third Sunday of Easter

Fourth Sunday of Easter

Fifth Sunday of Easter

Sixth Sunday of Easter

Ascension of the Lord
     (Fortieth day, Sixth Thursday of Easter)

Seventh Sunday of Easter

Day of Pentecost

SEASON AFTER PENTECOST (ORDINARY TIME)*

Trinity Sunday
(First Sunday after Pentecost)

Propers 4 — 28 (9 — 33)
(Second through Twenty-Sixth Sunday after Pentecost)

Proper 29 [34]   Sunday between November 20 and November 26
(Reign of Christ or Christ the King, Last Sunday
after Pentecost)

SPECIAL DAYS

February 2 — Presentation of the Lord

March 25 — Annunciation of the Lord

May 31 — Visitation of Mary to Elizabeth

September 14 — Holy Cross

November 1 — All Saints

Fourth Thursday of November (U.S.), Second Monday of October (Can.) — Thanksgiving Day

* Note: Since Easter is a moveable feast, it can occur as early as March 22 and as late as April 25. When Easter is early, it encroaches on the Sundays after the Epiphany, reducing their number, as necessary, from as many as nine to as few as four. In similar fashion, the date of Easter determines the number of Sunday Propers after Pentecost. When Easter is as early as March 22, the numbered Proper for the Sunday following Trinity Sunday is Proper 3.

The Propers in [brackets] indicate the Proper numbering system of the Roman Catholic Church and The Anglican Church of Canada.